IT'S *NOT* A GLASS CEILING
IT'S A STICKY FLOOR

Free Yourself from the Hidden Behaviors
Sabotaging Your Career Success

Rebecca Shambaugh

New York   Chicago   San Francisco   Lisbon   London   Madrid   Mexico City
Milan   New Delhi   San Juan   Seoul   Singapore   Sydney   Toronto

The *McGraw·Hill* Companies

1 2 3 4 5 6 7 8 9 0   DOC/DOC   0 9 8 7

ISBN-13: 978-0-07-149394-9
ISBN-10: 0-07-149394-8

McGraw-Hill books are available at special quantity discounts to use as premiums and sales promotions, or for use in corporate training programs. For more information, please write to the Director of Special Sales, Professional Publishing, McGraw-Hill, Two Penn Plaza, New York, NY 10121-2298. Or contact your local bookstore.

Contents

Acknowledgments

THE GREATEST JOYS and inspiring moments in writing this book can be attributed to the extraordinary and accomplished people who supported me during this process. I have always believed, as it happened in writing this book, that it takes a team to accomplish your dreams, and I was fortunate to have such an accomplished, dedicated, and supportive team around me.

First, I want to acknowledge both of my parents, Max and Mary Lou Shambaugh and my stepmother Sylvia Shambaugh—who were instrumental in shaping my values, which meant having the courage and confidence to live your dreams and pursue what you believe and are purposely driven to be and do. Special gratitude to my sister Cindy Armbruster and brother Mark Shambaugh who have been an enormous support system through their special love, adventures we have shared, and the true joy of laughing and supporting each other during the cycle of our lives. And to my dear and inspiring nieces and nephew, Nicole, Bryce, Morgen, Madison, and Sierra, who in many ways were an inspiration for writing this book as I hope they will be leaders in the years to come.

One of the gifts of writing this book was being able to connect with so many wonderful and supportive people—all of whom had helpful experiences, insights, and wisdom. One of my greatest challenges and deepest regrets was not being able to include all of the great thoughts and insights that I gathered over the course of my writing. Know that your knowledge and contributions were valued and inspirational in every way.

Thanks to Gail Ross Literacy Agency which understood the value and timeliness of getting this message out to the business community and women particularly. My genuine thanks to Stacey Zoe, Award Winning Journalist, for her tremendous help and support in editing several publications and her great support in editing my book proposal, all of which led me to a place where I was ready to take on the book itself. And special thanks to Eileen Gunn, freelance writer and editor, who supported me in the overall editing of the book and provided helpful guidance along the way.

Special thanks to Herb Schaffner, my editor at McGraw-Hill, whom I thoroughly enjoyed working with from the early days of the book to its completion. Thank you for challenging me to write a final manuscript that showed up as my own voice and was worthy, useful, and practical for readers to consume.

Through the years and still today, I have been truly fortunate to have an extraordinary team of people at SHAMBAUGH who were dedicated and supportive in building our company and have kept it thriving over the last sixteen years. Their valuable insights, frankness, and accomplished depth of knowledge were instrumental in pulling this book together. I am blessed to have a supportive team of people who have been vital in helping to continue to grow and sustain SHAMBAUGH's Women in Leadership and Learning (WILL) mission. Their dedication, expertise, and contributions, all at a level of high quality and exemplary standards, have allowed SHAMBAUGH to have the impact it has had for so many wonderful women whom we have had the opportunity to support in furthering their leadership. Special thanks to Lynette Demarest for her wealth of ideas and meticulous review of each chapter and to Mary Alice Callahan who provided ideas and inspiration when I needed a fresh approach or perspective. A special thanks to Peg Clarkson, Jenny Stisher, Maureen Early, and Elizabeth Blevins for their insights, feedback, and wisdom that were so needed in this book.

A special thanks to Helen Thomas, who once told me that I needed to write this book. I told Helen that I had never written a book but she said simply, "you have something to say so you should start writing," and I did. And to Frances Hesselbein, a woman who I met serendipitously when checking out of my hotel in San Francisco in 1999 after we both had spoken at the same leadership conference. We immediately connected and she picked up on my passion and vision for women leaders. From that day forward Francis has been a dear mentor and a source of my energy to pursue my vision and get the word out through my book.

My deepest gratitude and respect for the members of SHAMBAUGH's Executive Summit—a wonderful and accomplished community of women who have in many ways been the wind beneath my wings and who provided tremendous support and energy throughout the entire process of writing this book.

There are also a number of dear friends and colleagues who have either participated in the book or who have believed and supported my vision and passion for it and inspired me in other ways. Special thanks to Anne Altman, Susan DeFife, Elizabeth Lewis, Tina Sung, Kathleen Alexander, Jim Lafond, Susan Colantuno, Mary Ann Fisher, Karla Leavelle, Leslie Tracey, Anne Hacket, Cindy Ingram, Doug Ingram, Kathy Clark, Deborah Shore, Lota Zoth, Christine Dingivan, Jan Cooper, April Young, and Dan Bannister for sharing your enthusiasm for life and your intentional support and friendship.

I also want to thank all the senior executives and CEOs I interviewed for this book. Thank you for your openness as well as the realistic perspectives and practical approaches which were invaluable.

Writing this book has provided me such rich and wonderful experiences—a memorable journey in my life. My hope is that this book will touch the hearts and minds of others as much as the process of writing this book has inspired me.

Introduction

We Have Come a Long Way, But Is It Good Enough?

THIS OUGHT TO be the decade of the woman leader. Look at the statistics: More than one-third of Fortune 500 managers are women. More than half of the graduates who earn multidisciplinary master's degrees are women. More women hold elected office than ever before, and 9 million more women than men voted in the last presidential election. When you also consider the fact that women now make more than 80 percent of all purchasing decisions, there's a good argument to be made that women already have a lot of power!

And yet, women still aren't the top leaders. Again, just look at the statistics: Women hold only 14.5 percent of Fortune 500 CEO positions. They represent barely 6 percent of the top earners on Fortune 500 executive teams, and fewer than one in seven women occupy board-of-director seats. Many of these statistics sound familiar as they relate to women abroad who hold executive and senior leadership positions. You would think that with all the progress women have made in shaping the business environment, there would be more women holding executive positions.

The foregone conclusion about this stalled state of affairs is that there is a *glass ceiling*. That is, others, usually men, are preventing women from rising to the top with limiting stereotypes, exclusive old-boy networks, and institutional or cultural biases that favor men. While that does still hold true in some organizations, it's important for women to look at what they might be doing, or not doing, to hold themselves back. I call these self-defeating or self-limiting actions the *sticky floors*. We all have certain attitudes, behaviors, or traits that stop us from doing something we could do, or worse, that cause others to view us as "not executive material."

Decades of research continue to prop up the *glass ceiling* theory. And I don't disagree that there are still cultural impediments in business and in society. But as I've worked with women and organizations for the last two decades to cultivate women leaders, I often see something else that is also part of this dilemma. I see women holding themselves back far more than society ever could. And they usually do it to themselves quite unknowingly. When I see women capable of executive suite leadership mired in middle management, I don't look for the *glass ceiling* anymore. Instead, I look for a *sticky floor*.

The Business Case for Great Leadership— A Timely Opportunity for Women Leaders

Catalyst, an independent research organization, conducted a study of 353 Fortune 500 companies and found that the companies with the most women in top management positions provided a total return to shareholders that was 35 percent better than in companies with more male-centric executive teams. This supports the notion that a more diverse spectrum of leadership perspectives, traits, and thinking really does drive bottom-line performance. Inclusion and diversity programs are not the "right" thing to do, so much as the "smart" thing to do. The most progressive and savvy companies in the United States and abroad appreciate that consciously cultivating a broader mix of leaders will make them better at meeting consumer demands and positioning themselves in the marketplace. And they will also be better able to take advantage of opportunities in a global and continuously evolving business world.

One statistic after another indicates that women are increasingly instrumental in strategy, decisionmaking, and leadership. So where are these women? It seems that many of the ones who should be storming the executive suite to influence important company-wide decisions are still somewhere down on the lower floors, taking direction from above.

What Does a Sticky Floor Look Like?

Like every other diligent schoolgirl, I learned that working hard and keeping your head down over your schoolbooks will win you high marks and recognition. I applied the same strategy when I started working by putting in long hours, staying on task, and being untiringly diligent. However, I eventually realized that what gets you to the head of the class doesn't necessarily land you the corner office. The things I learned in kindergarten were the very things that could make my feet stick to the floor.

Women who believe that success is earned by meeting deadlines and staying under budget are mistakenly clinging to inappropriate career strategies. In today's workplace, everyone is expected to meet their goals. To be considered leadership material, you need to step out of the "worker bee" box and, well . . . lead!

When I talk with women passed over for promotions or executive-level jobs, I often see problems that are their own creation, such as the one above. This is good news for women though, because while you can't single-handedly alter broad societal views and cultural taboos, you can learn from your mistakes and make changes in yourself. A sticky floor is a better problem to have than a glass ceiling because you can pull yourself free of the sticky floor, or see it before you get stuck, and begin climbing to the highest rungs of the corporate ladder. Know that we all have sticky floors—men and women alike. However, my organization has been able to identify unique patterns of behaviors, beliefs, and assumptions that unknowingly will hold back accomplished and smart women from achieving their greatest potential.

After years of working in senior human resources jobs, I left the corporate world to launch SHAMBAUGH Leadership, a consulting firm that provides leadership and organizational development expertise to Fortune 500 clients around the world. I also created a division especially for women, Women in Leadership and Learning (WILL), which is dedicated to the research, development, advancement, and retention of women leaders and executives across the globe.

What Are the Sticky Floors?

For the past 10 years, through WILL, I have been helping organizations turn women with leadership potential into senior-level leaders. A large part of this work has been helping the women to recognize and address any beliefs, assumptions, and self-defeating behaviors that have held them back. This does not mean that women are always stuck and are not talented. Quite the contrary. However, rising to greater levels of influence, responsibility, visibility, and decisionmaking, requires us to view things from a broader and more diverse perspective. And to realize that what made us successful in our careers so far may not be the best equation for continued success. When we are not aware of what we do and the impact it has, or apply the right techniques and skills to overcome certain obstacles, we run into the sticky floors which can limit our ability to achieve our ideal career goals. These sticky floors fall into a handful of categories that I will address chapter by chapter in this book. The chapters will not only help you to explore where you are on each of these, but will also provide proven techniques, strategies, and skills to avoid getting stuck or, if you are stuck, to help you get unstuck.

They are as follows:

- Balancing Your Work-Life
- Embracing "Good Enough"
- Making the Break
- Making Your Words Count
- Forming Your Own Board of Directors
- Capitalizing on Your Political Savvy
- Asking for What You Want

One or more of these sticky floors bogs everyone down over the course of their careers. Staying in the corporate world for too long eventually emerged as a sticky floor for me. I wanted to run my own business, and at some point I finally had to ask myself, if not now, when? It was always going to be comfortable here (wherever here might be at the moment), so I decided now was as good a time as any. I did a risk factor analysis: I knew I had enough money in the bank and potential clients lined up to get started on my own. The only thing that I had to do was take a deep breath and walk out the door and, I did!

How Do We Get Stuck?

Women don't pick up these limiting behaviors and beliefs overnight. They allow them to evolve over a long period of time—years or even decades.

Some women have been taught, or have taught themselves (or both), not to aspire to stretch beyond their comfort zone. Others feel that they have worked so hard to get where they are, that they couldn't possibly get to that last executive-level rung without changing their lifestyle or burning out. Some look at the women above them and believe they must be frazzled and unhappy given all they have on their plates—though, in most cases, they are actually content and satisfied. And still others assume they aren't valued or accepted by the inner circle of male leaders at their company, even while these women fail to reach out to these colleagues for support. Finally, others don't believe it's possible to achieve a healthy work-life balance in the highest-level jobs.

All of these things can be boiled down to two key things: false assumptions and lack of information. As you read this book, I'll help you to take a good look at those assumptions and provide you with lots of new information! Take a few moments and invest in "you." Take this opportunity to look within yourself and see where you might be holding yourself back from achieving your fullest potential—which might just be the executive suite. You might find, as I did, that many of your assumptions are illusions and if you don't step out of your comfort zone now to challenge your old, self-limiting points of view and behaviors, you may be your own greatest obstacle to reaching fulfillment. Know that you do have more control of your destiny than you sometimes think you do!

What's a Woman to Do if She Wants to Rise Off the Sticky Floor and Prosper in Her Career?

Yes, I know perfectly well that women are forced to haul more than their fair share of societal or cultural weight up the career ladder. But, the upside is richer experiences, deeper knowledge, and stronger empathies that they can draw on to solve problems, strategize, and inspire people—if they learn to make use of that advantage rather than seeing it as a hindrance.

You do this by looking inward, as I mentioned earlier. The trick to getting unstuck is realizing you are stuck and then formulating a plan for shaking loose the problem and acting on that plan—and that's what this book will help you do. This book looks at the many ways women hold themselves back. And, in every instance, moving forward begins with *self-awareness*.

Strong leaders—women and men—are able to honestly assess their strengths and weaknesses. They also are very good at knowing their values and setting goals that support those values. They use this knowledge to make career decisions and to develop leadership styles that play up their strengths and compensate for their shortcomings. Being true to themselves is critical to their success and fulfillment. This book will illustrate my journey of leadership and how some of my greatest challenges, that seemed obstacles at the time, became my greatest leadership moments. They were my opportunities to learn, grow, and take accountability for my own success and happiness. I am not and will never be perfect, but I learned along the way that the sticky floors are obstacles and sometimes illusions that we can overcome. This book will show you several ways to do your own self-evaluations, to clarify your goals, and to align your goals with your own strengths and values.

Don't let self-doubt get the best of you; you have strengths! To indulge in positive stereotypes for a moment, women are generally inclined to possess some of the most in-demand traits for leaders today, such as a collaborative leadership style, creativity, good intuition, an ability to coordinate seemingly disparate ideas, and a focus on relationships. These are the very things business schools and consulting firms tell us leaders need in order to run today's organizations. The opportunity, yet challenge, for many of us is being able to make that shift within ourselves—to see, believe, and show up with the powerful leadership gifts that we possess. The time is now and the world is ready.

But no matter how great your strengths are, critical shortcomings can undermine them and keep you out of the executive suite or prevent you from reaching your career goals. So it's important to know all aspects of who you are.

In your career, as in everything else, you have choices. I am glad you have made the choice to read this book, and allow it to help you look within yourself, to find the courage to step out of your comfort zone, and to learn the important skills missing from your executive portfolio.

As more and more change comes to our world of work—from technological innovation, to increasing diversity across the United States and the globe, to the coming wave of baby-boomer retirements—there is going to be a leadership vacuum. Women are well positioned to fill this void and to be a vital resource for addressing new demands from customers all over the world. The question to ask yourself is: How can I become one of the many women poised for this opportunity?

Why This Book?

My hope is that after reading this book you'll know how to recognize and tap into your own power, how to identify the things that keep you from moving forward, and how to take responsibility for your own success.

So read on, and then identify the leadership position you want and go for it. Be clear on what you envision for yourself and know how you'll invest in your talents to get there.

And remember, once women free themselves from the sticky floors, there is no glass ceiling. Instead, the sky is the limit!

Chapter 1

Know Yourself—Be Yourself

"You must create your own roadmap to your chosen destination based on your values, beliefs, and strengths."

The Beginning...

Things started out nicely enough. Shortly after graduating from Purdue University in the late 70s, I was offered a job as one of the first female managers on a General Motors production floor. But once I started, it didn't take long (by which I mean mere hours) to realize that I should have considered more carefully the role of gender in the workplace, and should have asked a few more questions during my job interview.

I arrived for my first day of work at 6:30 a.m. full of energy and excitement. I knew nothing about cars, except how to pull into a gas station and fill up my tank. That was not one of the job requirements, however. Instead I was expected to learn the 120 auto parts they used on this assembly line—and I had to succeed in an environment that had sent three previous managers packing in just 10 months.

I knew when I walked into the plant, and everything and everybody stopped, that I was in for a challenge. It was like one of those

1

hushed movie moments. Everyone looked up and stared at me. At first, I wondered what was wrong with my appearance—did I have toilet paper dragging from my shoe or, worse yet, hanging from beneath my skirt? A glance down confirmed nothing was wrong; a glance up confirmed that I was the only woman in a sea of Teamster men.

The production manager waved me off with, "Good luck. See you at six!" By 9 a.m., the shop steward had come by with the first grievance against me. One of my quality control guys said he missed his coffee break because of a defect in one of the parts he caught running off the line. He had not missed a coffee break in 10 years and made it clear he wouldn't miss another one again. Later, after going through the third grievance procedure that morning, someone lit a fire in a garbage can in my department. By the end of the day, I had accumulated a record 25 grievances. Not much else could go wrong, right?

That afternoon, I walked into my first management meeting. Seventeen men in suits looked up. Seventeen mouths dropped open, and seventeen pens fell from their hands. I placed my meticulously prepared reports on the table in front of me, only to hear this: "Becky, you take notes."

That Which Doesn't Kill You...

This experience was one of the greatest leadership development programs I could ever put myself in. At the tender age of 24, I had to learn how to build a diverse spectrum of relationships, to effectively manage the blue-collar men who were so different from me, and to play the middleman in negotiations between the union and management staff. You can bet my social and emotional intelligence were stretched daily—and I loved it. However, after three years and my fifth promotion, I realized that I had reached a peak at GM.

I could have stayed on and advanced to be a head of plant production or even head of headquarters for human resources in Detroit, but in the long term, I didn't want to stay in manufacturing and production.

Fortunately I had a new opportunity presented to me. I was offered a job more aligned with my long-term goals at Amax Inc., a billion-dollar energy company, where I worked for its coal mining division located in Indianapolis. It provided me with broader human resources responsibilities, more opportunities to work with senior executives, and the chance to rotate through jobs that taught me about business activities company-wide. I had a supportive and experienced group of colleagues, mostly men, who served as helpful mentors along the way. I was fortunate to have a boss who was receptive to my ideas and willing to put me in a variety of diverse projects—all leading me to a promotion in my first year.

Then—4 years later, to my great surprise—I got a pink slip. I was shocked and in denial. Despite watching layoffs happen to others, I never thought I would be one of the victims.

How could this happen? Everything had gone so well. Like so many others in this situation, I was struck with self-doubt. I wondered about my abilities and my skills. And the problem was worse than it seemed. It was a bad economy, with a local unemployment rate of 15 percent—and Indianapolis wasn't exactly a booming metropolis in good times. What would I do?

Standing in the unemployment line with 50 folks who had many more years of experience than me, who were looking for the same type of jobs I was seeking, an important realization struck me. Job opportunities in that town were slim, and no one was going to single me out from that long line of talented and credentialed executives to hand me a golden opportunity. I needed to create change for myself and take responsibility for my future. I could use this as an opportunity to pursue my dream job. This was a chance to push out of my comfort zone, take a risk, and take control of my destiny. If I didn't, I would most likely be visiting the unemployment line for some time.

I knew this was what I needed to do to solve my immediate problem of getting a job. But I also had a glimmer of understanding that I was taking an important step toward building a career.

This was the beginning of my appreciation that it's important to have a vision of who you want to be and to continually take small, mindful steps toward that vision.

I began thinking of my job search as a process for self-evaluation and set out to learn about all the different aspects of who I was. What were my strengths, beliefs, fears, and motivations? I decided to pull over for about six months and take a hard look at what I wanted to do, as well as at my key drivers and decide how they would help to determine my next job. I found a book about managing your career and there was an exercise on identifying and living your values that I began to fill out. What was fascinating was that the top five values I had listed—relationships, creating and building new business opportunities, taking risks, continually learning, and helping others—were the very things that had motivated me in my first two jobs.

I then began to reflect back on the conversations I'd had with my father, Max Shambaugh, at the kitchen table when I was a little girl. I was always fascinated by the fact that he had built a third-generation family business into one of the largest construction companies in the country. My father instilled in me an approach to work that I still value today. Specifically, he encouraged me to take risks but to be prudent about it, to build on my strengths and relationships, and to follow through on things I'm passionate about.

I used these things I had discovered about myself to focus and expand my job search. And within six months I had three job offers—two in the Midwest and one on the East Coast. I ended up taking the job in Washington, D.C., as head of human resources for the corporate headquarters of Fairchild Industries.

It was a darn good decision that would set me on the long-term career path I really wanted for myself. I took the position knowing it was a leap of faith to move to a new city in order to accept a job for which I was not totally qualified. But the job at Fairchild had everything I was looking for and I knew that whether or not it worked out, at least I was taking it for the right reasons. When making the decision on whether or not to move, I asked myself what would be the worst thing that could happen and I realized that I had nothing to lose and much to gain. The job that would provide the right stretch and allow me to form a greater level of inner competence and confidence down the road.

By going through that decision-making process to determine my next move, I learned that knowing yourself first and then having the focus, courage, and commitment to take action toward your goals is the key to success, as well as to satisfaction and fulfillment. However, let me emphasize that there is not always a linear path to success, even when you know your goals and have your roadmap charted out. This is why it's so critical to be aware of the person you are—your core values, beliefs, strengths, and weaknesses. You need that self-knowledge to navigate the twists, bumps, and detours you'll no doubt encounter along the way.

Does This Situation Sound Familiar?

Have you had points in your career where you felt perpetually exhausted and burnt out, or where you knew your performance was not at its peak because the fit wasn't quite right, or where you were handed that awful pink slip and felt at a loss about what to do next? Maybe you're there right now. Take comfort in knowing you are not alone. Everyone hits a career cul-de-sac now and then.

The trick to finding your way out is to avoid getting caught up in a sense of crisis (a very sticky floor). Instead, appreciate that you are poised at an opportunity for change. Think about the kinds of changes you would like and consider how you would go about making at least one of them happen.

If you've never done it before, take some time out to go through the kind of self-evaluation and life planning I did. You don't need the six months I could afford to take as a young woman with plump savings and few responsibilities. Even one evening session of intense career planning can get you started. There are resources right in this book to help you, and myriad resources online, in other books, and with people like career coaches if you'd like to go further.

Know Yourself, Be Yourself

So, why all this fuss about knowing and being yourself?

I believe that great leadership is *so much* about knowing who you are. Successful leaders know their strengths, weaknesses, beliefs, motivations, and intentions.

In short, self-knowledge is the starting point for absolutely everything else; the successes you want and, equally important, the setbacks you're bound to encounter.

I spend a lot of time talking with women who are in a transition, who feel like they have no control of their destiny, or who feel frustrated or ready to give up because they did not win some plum job for which they recently interviewed. I know how frustrating this can be, but at the end of the day, I tell women that the key to coming out ahead in these types of situations is to have a steady, reliable self-image to fall back on. Once you have that grounded and mindful self-awareness, you can channel it into whatever you want to be.

The fundamental questions for all of us are: Who do you want to be and how do you manifest that in your life and work?

There are hundreds of books on this topic in bookstores and probably on your shelf at home or in the office. But, there is more to it than just knowing yourself—there's also *being* yourself.

Identifying and being yourself is critical for great leaders and a chief reason why they succeed or derail. I believe that the ability to know and be yourself has a direct correlation to your ability to have an impact on things around you and create results that matter to you and your team, customers, organization, family, and community.

Having a critical awareness of your motivations and intentions channels your behaviors in the right direction and ensures that you are always taking the right small steps toward those big-picture goals. Maybe you want that next promotion, or to influence key customers on a proposal, or have a difficult conversation with your boss about why you can't take on that next project. Knowing why you do or don't want to do these things, and where you ultimately want them to get you, will help you to motivate yourself and persevere.

The exercises and liberating solutions I will provide, along with my story and those of other women, will help you to develop this self-knowledge that is fundamental to successful leadership. This book should help you to know yourself, understand your strengths and weaknesses, get clear on your goals, face your greatest fears, and use this new inventory of knowledge to develop a personal action plan.

Along the way you will discern, assess, and perhaps reframe your personal belief system, break free of old patterns that are undermining your success, and learn how to take control of your future.

How Do You Get to Know Yourself?

Leaders who don't have internal self-awareness peak soon after they've gotten the top jobs; or worse, derail their careers before they even get close. Why? When you know who you are and are true to that, your actions and reactions are consistent. As a result, others feel more comfortable approaching you and more willing to place their trust in you, share their views with you, and support your ideas. When you know who you are, you feel and project inner confidence, which enables you to build credibility and identify with others. You are the leader who projects a sense of stability during crisis, change, debate, or conflict. You project a centeredness that others pick up and, in most cases, create this magical focus and alignment for others.

On a personal level, the impact of not knowing yourself is that you might take the wrong job, or make other decisions you'll regret down the road. You might make ill-considered choices that leave you having to repair an important relationship, or that undermine other people's trust in you. Knowing how you want to appear to others and then being that person, versus being someone else, is critical to every leader's credibility, influence, satisfaction, and overall fulfillment.

In the early part of my career, I listened, watched, and got to know people who rose to high levels of leadership and success. I observed that, aside from being competent in their field, they had something else in common. They actually took time out to examine themselves. This allowed them to access their strengths and intentions when important opportunities and challenges presented themselves. They also applied these insights to the daily onslaught of difficult decisions every executive faces. Finally, they knew their weaknesses, and that helped them to understand and manage the assumptions and behavior patterns that could get them into trouble when they were under stress or pressure.

Lydia Thomas, Ph.D., president and CEO of Mitretek, a not-for-profit research center in Falls Church, Virginia, observes, "As a leader, you need to be your own person—you can't pretend." She points out, quite correctly, that no one can act all the time. "People should know what they are getting when they get you and you should be happy about what you are providing to others."

The next chapter will take you through the roadmap for personal discovery that I have incorporated into my own life. Even if you are already familiar with some of these areas of introspection, it is still important to reflect on them from time to time because the one thing constant in life is change, and it's important to revisit our values and goals as the context of our lives change. If they're new to you, they should help you to look at yourself, your day-to-day work, and your career in a more clear-eyed way.

Chapter 2

Taking Action for Knowing and Being Yourself

The Value of Self-Awareness

In the first chapter, I talked about the importance of knowing your-self and the notion that if you don't have that awareness it will be hard for you to know where you might get *stuck*. So now, I want to build on that concept and talk about the "how" of knowing yourself.

Over the past 16 years, my organization has worked with thou-sands of leaders from a cross-section of industries, such as financial services, technology, pharmaceuticals, manufacturing, biotech, lodg-ing, retail, nonprofit, government, and professional services. We are in the business of helping people learn and develop as great leaders. To do that, SHAMBAUGH starts from the premise that leadership is not just *what you do*, but also *who you are*.

SHAMBAUGH's research indicates, over and over again, that the number one factor that distinguishes highly effective leaders is self-awareness. We are seeing that more and more organizations are rec-ognizing the value of self-awareness and are increasing the opportunities and experiences to enhance the self-awareness of their leaders and executives, which can have a positive impact on their level of performance, commitment, focus, and with the alignment between the individual's personal goals and those of the organization.

We use guided self-assessments to have leaders understand who they are and recognize the impact they have on others. Our goal is not to turn them into leaders, but rather to create an environment where they learn to be more aware of their own behaviors/traits and to understand how their intentions and actions can make them either assets or liabilities to themselves and their organization. Once they have that level of awareness, they are equipped to accept accountability for their behavior and impact, and they have what they need to make leaders of themselves.

Taking Action For Knowing and Being Yourself

Here is an example of someone who learned and applied how to reframe her self image and belief system. She was a successful physician and saw herself as competently independent. She had all the expertise to work independently and make all the right decisions.

While she was passionate about her profession and the kind of work she did, she worked long hours and had no personal life. She realized she had to make a decision—did she want to stay in the role as a physician and give up her work/life balance or did she want to reshape her role working in an industry where she might actually have a better personal life. She had always believed that she would be a great physician and wondered how she could ever reshape her role into something as different as working as a leader in industry.

When she received a job offer from a major bio tech company, she decided to take on the new challenge of heading up an important area of their research department. She soon realized that what would make her successful in her new job was quite different in her past role as a physician. Soon after she joined the company, she was promoted to a leadership position. She quickly learned that she needed to rely on others to make decisions and to work in a collaborative way. She was responsible for managing a small team of individuals which required her to be on top of their day to day performance, communications, and overall development. This was quite a contrast from being in the operating room and going from one crisis to another.

To make this transition, her organization suggested she go through our Women in Leadership and Learning (WILL) program and work with one of our executive coaches. As a result of their experiences and structured introspection process she was able to reframe the image she had of herself in terms of her career and her inner belief system. Overtime she began to tap into other areas of her potential and was promoted to a senior vice president of her organization. If you know yourself it is much easier to reframe your belief system and develop your full potential.

Finding Meaning—It's Connection to Self-Awareness

Taking the time and having the courage to examine and be honest about your own experiences, strengths, weaknesses, and other intrinsic motivations is an essential ingredient for leaders to be successful in reaching their fullest potential. It all starts with building self-awareness and continually checking in to see how these evolve and change. I see many leaders in the early parts of their career who are trying to establish themselves, determine the best path to go, and define what really excites them, motivates them, and brings them the greatest satisfaction in their work. While these factors may drive success for them for a while, they are unable to sustain that success. They may realize that their career aspirations change or they are changing as a person from a values and lifestyle perspective.

A landmark study in the Harvard Business Review, "Discovering Your Authentic Leadership," by Bill George, Peer Sims, Andrew McLean, and Diana Mayer, indicates that sometimes we see leaders continue to strive for success in tangible ways such as money, status, or number of stock options and then the company they work for is sold or reorganized. They lose their power or stock options, and have no stability or true sense of identity or purpose. It is not easy to lead our lives based on constant external pressures or expectations from others. And sometimes we feel guilty or hesitant to say no to a new job for fear of what others will say or do. Taking on new roles or staying in the same one that is not aligned with who we are, what's important to us, or what we feel we deserve, can lead to dissatisfaction, burnout, and undue stress within ourselves. No matter how successful or on track we think we are, it is important for all of us at some point in our career to check in and ask ourselves the sometimes difficult question, "Where do I find happiness and fulfillment?" Are you like the proverbial hamster spinning on the wheel and not going anywhere, or are you engaged in a career and life that is meaningful, brings you great satisfaction, and is aligned with your strengths, values, and career-life dreams?

Finding meaning and purpose in our career calls for becoming self-aware, but it is not an overnight process. It requires commitment and time for self-reflection to look honestly and deeply within yourself and to reach out to others to gain their perspective. The latter can be harder because others rarely see us exactly as we see ourselves, but it's invaluable to be able to compare the impact you're actually having on others to the impact you are aiming for and that you believe you are achieving. Studies from the Center for Creative Leadership indicate that the most common reason why executives fail is their inability to grasp other people's perspective. So I am always an advocate of soliciting feedback from others—it's a wonderful gift executives aren't privy to unless they ask for it.

Your Career and Fulfillment Starts with You!

Leadership, as we discussed, starts with knowing who you are. It calls for a commitment for you to become critically aware of your makeup from all perspectives and dimensions (strengths, weaknesses, values, internal and external motivations) and then shaping a career path and development plan to get there. Sometimes we find ourselves in a place where our job is not fulfilling, we are frustrated or even doubting ourselves. We are handed a career plan by our boss and it's not really where we want to go or be, or it is not playing to our strengths. So much of that can lead to internal conflict and dissatisfaction. Don't forget that a development plan should be coactive with you and your boss. We can sometimes get ourselves in a hole or on the wrong track if we expect the organization to shape and form our career direction. The more aware you are of yourself, the more equipped you will be to take the right steps, have the "right" conversation, and take control of your own career destiny.

The Process of Getting to Know Yourself

At SHAMBAUGH, we have a number of integrated tools, solutions, and programs we use to help leaders develop key insights into their emotions, ways of thinking, habits, character traits, and results, and to help them apply those insights to their work. We hope these exercises invite people to see their work from a new point of view and themselves in a different way. Below are abbreviated, self-directed versions of some of these exercises to get you started on building your own self-awareness.

To begin, I will take you through a process where you will evaluate your behaviors and skills and see which serve your current ambitions and which might be holding you back. You'll also look at your self-image and some of your beliefs, and compare and contrast your view of yourself to views of others around you. And you'll have a chance to consider whether some of the assumptions or beliefs that served you well in your early career may be holding you back as you try to climb higher.

Then you'll examine your values—what are the things you most want to contribute to and get back from your personal and professional lives? Finally, you'll lay out a vision of the person you want to grow into over the course of your career. You'll look at how the things you want to achieve align with your values, and how your strengths and weaknesses can foster or undermine your goals.

Finally, I'll help you to craft a plan for moving forward with all this new information so that if your career is out of whack with your values, you can move to align it better, and you can start enhancing the strengths and shoring up the weaknesses that are most important to your success.

A Look at Strengths and Weaknesses in the Executive Suite

The higher you move in an organization, the more important it is to assess the dynamics of any new role, reassess your skill set, and think in broader terms about the appropriate traits, skills, and strengths you are trying to achieve. An executive vice president who is one or two levels away from being the CEO has different, probably broader, responsibilities than a mid-level manager overseeing a small department, and she is expected to adapt herself and her skills to this higher profile situation.

Here's a hint: When they finally offer you an assistant, it's not only appropriate, but expected that someone else will make your appointments and travel plans. You have more important things to do with your time. If you fail to learn to delegate the small stuff, it sends the message that you don't see yourself as an important thought leader and other people won't see you that way either.

The strengths and traits that got you to where you are, such as getting results, being detail oriented, being process focused, or a team player, are more of a recipe for being a good middle manager than an executive-suite executive. In contrast, executive-level leaders need to think strategically, have a vision for their organization and people, lead complex change, and build strategic and collaborative relationships inside and outside the organization. To advance to the executive level, you need to develop these skills and traits, and in a sense repackage yourself to draw attention to them. I have coached a number of women advancing to the executive suite that it is essential to really know your strengths and be able to demonstrate them, so you will stand above the crowd in what you do best. Even if that strength is 10 percent of a new job you're taking, lead with that strength so you have an anchor and a greater sense of confidence. Seeing yourself as executive potential and acting that way is part of the game. This calls for an inventory of what you need to develop, and what you need to continue or stop doing, to build that outer and inner image.

It is important to reinforce that no one is going to excel at everything. Many women at this juncture in their career instinctively try to be all things to all people when in fact it is more about narrowing in on the skills and traits that have the greatest impact for you and your organization.

Take me as an example. I'm not the best at developing training programs, but that's okay; I have hired far more competent people to do that job for SHAMBAUGH. I bring more value developing the right relationships, maintaining the vision for the company, and keeping the organization on a strategic path.

Below is a process that will help you to focus on those areas where you need to excel, where you may be falling short, and where you can hold steady based on your role and the impact you are trying to have.

Your Alignment with Your Organization

How well aligned are your abilities and interests with your organization's goals and values? Answering the following questions will help to determine just that.

- What behaviors and attributes are valued in your organization?
- Based on where your organization is headed, what abilities will it need in its leaders over the next two to five years?
- What skills and behaviors will you need to bring continued value to your organization and succeed in your ideal role?
- How can you make the most of your strengths to fill those needs?
- Where will you need to shore up your weaknesses to round out what you bring to your job?

After doing this exercise you should see a strong alignment between your organization's current and future needs and your strengths. You want to make sure that you don't wind up in a situation where you're striving to fit your square peg in a round hole.

If you're beginning to see that your abilities and inclinations are not well aligned with the organization, then you need to start a process for determining what it would take to get in the groove or to look at the pros and cons of staying versus leaving.

A Few Pointers

- Discover your natural inclinations by looking at your organization's mission-critical behaviors to see what excites you or gives you a sense of purpose or satisfaction.
- Don't spend a lot of time on your weaknesses unless they are critical to proving yourself for that next job. For example, you can make up for less in-depth knowledge about finance by having a good relationship with the CFO and being able to consult him or her on your financial decisions. However, this would be a fatal flaw if you'd be expected to join the finance committee in your next role. And, in that case, you should find the time to take a financial course, perhaps as a weekend or weeklong executive education course at a good business school.

Using a 360-Degree Evaluation to Determine the Strengths You Have and the Strengths You'll Need

Others see you far more objectively than you can ever see yourself. This is why I have always found that the best way to find out about your strengths and shortcomings is to ask for feedback from those you trust to be honest with you. Feedback from the right people establishes a connection between what we think we do and our effect on people. Some people will shy away from direct feedback for fear of being too shocked or taken aback by what they hear. But, in my own leadership experience, I've decided that difficult feedback really is better than no feedback at all. I would rather not be left on my own to figure out what others are thinking and feeling about me.

Here is a four-step process I recommend for getting the feedback that will serve you well:

1. **Identify behaviors and attributes that matter.** Determine the behaviors and attributes that are necessary for you to be successful in your role. These should include the key business objectives for your group and should be put in the context of your company culture. I encourage you to think big and consider what you want to demonstrate about yourself in this role to show you're ready for bigger things—maybe even the executive suite.

2. **Determine who can provide meaningful feedback.** It's called a 360-degree evaluation because it's supposed to include perceptions of you from all sides. So make a mental list of your key stakeholders which includes your direct reports, boss, peers, customers, suppliers, or any other members of your leadership team. The key here is to find people who have had several experiences with you, and who can give feedback that will help you to improve your performance, leadership ability, and relationships. As hard as it may be, don't steer away from those who may provide you with difficult feedback.

3. **Solicit feedback.** This process can be handled in several different ways, such as anonymous surveys or one-on-one interviews. I often recommend hiring a coach to work with you on a questionnaire and process for soliciting the feedback. A coach can also pull it all together into a summary report to share with you and help you make sense of it.

4. **Develop your action plan.** Some feedback will be a happy surprise. You might not be aware of some of the things you've been doing that people really value and appreciate. On the other hand, no one is perfect, so people will also see shortcomings or behaviors that they believe undermine your

effectiveness. The key is to focus on a few critical behaviors that have the strongest weighting in your success and to look at the strongest trends and patterns—the things you hear over and over rather than the one-off comments. Once you've gotten a clear picture of what's good and what needs improvement, work with a coach or mentor who can help you develop a plan that might include cross-assignments, mentoring by experts in areas where you come up short, or formal development tools and programs from inside or outside your organization.

Managing and Leveraging Your Feedback— Make It Count

Once you have people offering their perceptions of you, you'll need to be open and accepting about what they have to say (and if you aren't, don't expect people to offer this feedback again). This isn't easy, but it's the greatest gift you can receive as an executive, or aspiring executive.

Self-Image: The Overlooked Success Factor

We spend so much of our career-planning time thinking about the hard, tactical stuff such as skills, experience, knowledge, goals, and performance, that we can forget how dramatically the softer stuff, like self-image, can impact our success. So next up, you're going to take a close look at what you think of yourself and why and how that self-image is fostering or impeding your ultimate success.

To get started, imagine you are sitting at dinner (table for one), and you ask yourself, "What sort of person am I?" You might respond, "I'm a fix-it person. I clean up other people's messes and botched projects." Or you might say, "I'm a department head type."

Now, if I were sitting across from you, I'd ask, "Why do you think you are a fixer? Why don't you think you're the CEO type?" I'd bet dessert it's because that's the role you've been assigned over and over again. It's a given that much of how we see the world and respond to experiences is based on a collection of beliefs we have about who we are.

But many people don't realize that these beliefs are a mixture of internal forces and things that others project onto us. Part of anyone's self-image is right on the money and part is misinformed by the collective influence of our own and other people's biases. The self-image that evolves from this belief system can work for you or be limiting, and it's usually a little of both. For example, you might believe you don't have the educational background to be what you want to be. Or you might believe that you're selfish if you spend a lot of time on yourself. But at some point you have to realize that you are the architect of who you are. And you need to take responsibility for your self-image.

So, for your next step on this road to self-discovery, I encourage you to look hard within yourself and identify those beliefs about yourself that might be limiting. We do this for the women who attend our Women in Leadership and Learning (WILL) program and they end up saying that it really helps them to identify reasons why they feel stuck in their career or, in some cases, they feel conflicted about their ambition.

At WILL, we ask women to draw a timeline of experiences and events that shaped their assumptions about their world and how they view themselves.

One of my huge life events was going into my father's office on Saturday mornings and letting him show me all the construction jobs and bids he was working on. I was amazed by how he did it. I also got to see him interact with the other people in his company—from his secretary to the supervisors and workers. As an adult I realized that he had a tremendous ability to build strong relationships with his employees and I understood that much of his success was accomplished by these people who believed in and trusted him. That has stayed with me and formed my principles and beliefs as an entrepreneur. And that lesson has played a big part in SHAMBAUGH's success.

After the women complete their lifeline exercise, they have some "ah-hah" moments of their own. Once they do that we ask them to dig deeper and identify any beliefs about themselves that are negative, but also no longer true (if they ever were to begin with). This helps them to understand where and how their self-perception can be needlessly limiting.

I love seeing the light bulb turn on as they begin to write down positive affirmations of who they really are or want to be. It's an important and powerful exercise that can open up new doors, and empower you to move beyond your own obstacles and start on a new, positive path.

Exercise: Create Your Own Lifeline

Here are some simple steps for creating a timeline for your own life:

1. Think about significant events in your life (from childhood to the present) and rate them on a scale of 1 to 10; 1 for severe challenges and 10 for great events.

   For example, losing a loved one would be rated a 1, while a great love or an adventurous trip abroad is rated a 10. A promotion at work could be an 8, 9, or 10, and the loss of a job might be a 3, depending on the emotional uplift or pain you experienced. These events don't have to be big or momentous, but should loom large in your memory and be formative.

2. Once you have a good timeline, answer the following questions for each event:

- What impact did the event have on your life?

- How did the event impact your leadership abilities?

- How did your values evolve as a result of the event?

- Did this event contribute to making you a great leader? If not, how did it shape you?

- What motivated you at these different points in your past? What motivates you today?

3. Once you have identified those key highs and lows, start to connect the dots. What do the highs have in common? The lows? Do they reaffirm a vision you have of yourself or tell you something about your values and motivations that hadn't occurred to you before?

4. If you can, turn to a trusted colleague, friend, or partner, and discuss your leadership journey. Ask them how they believe the dots connect and why. Ask them which of their perceptions of you have made sense in the context of these events. And ask them what new perceptions they have about you as a result. Then think about or talk about what these findings tell you about where you want to go from here.

Reframing Your Beliefs

Like anything, any lifelong habits and beliefs that you know are not working for you can be difficult but important to address. Our brain can become hardwired in certain beliefs and assumptions, which can make it hard to change. It takes considerable effort and commitment to rewire our counterproductive or less helpful beliefs, assumptions, and patterns of behaviors. It takes persistence, more than a little will, and some well-timed help from other people around you.

I will never forget an event that fundamentally reshaped my inner belief system. I was introverted and shy all the way through my teenage years. Presenting in front of the class or speaking to an assembly was like having my wisdom teeth pulled out. I forced myself to show up and do it, but it was painful. I always had these fears that I would not be prepared, would flub up, people would be bored, and felt that I didn't deserve that level of attention on *me*.

As I progressed in my career, I became good at avoiding speaking obligations as much as I could, until close to 15 years ago when I was asked to speak about leadership to a large audience of community leaders at a major conference in Washington, D.C. By that point, I'd spent 10 years cultivating an expertise on leadership and promoting myself, indeed building my business on that expertise.

Nevertheless, I drove alone to the conference, anguishing about my talk, my knees shaking. I called Maureen, one of my business partners, and shared with her how anxious I was. She said, "Becky, I don't get it. They picked you because you are the expert in this area. In fact, you know more about this topic than they do and they are paying you a good fee to come out and talk. That should be enough for you to believe that they are coming to the conference out of respect for you and a desire to hear your perspective and firsthand knowledge based on your years of practice developing leaders."

I listened and it struck me that I never thought that way about myself, but if my partner Maureen did, then others just might feel the same way.

Hearing my business partner share her strong beliefs about me helped me to gain a greater level of inner confidence and belief about myself. I managed to present that morning and felt more comfortable and at ease than I ever had in front of an audience. All eyes were on me and people were engaged and asking questions—questions that I could actually answer. I found myself being the person my business partner described. I felt very comfortable, and that was the starting point for a new truth about myself as a public speaker.

It took years and one crucial conversation for me to understand that my unease was rooted in my continuing perception of myself as being shy. I didn't see myself as a speaker, so I dreaded speaking. Now I speak two or three times a week and enjoy connecting with large and small audiences on a topic about which I'm passionate and knowledgeable.

From that experience, I learned once again that to reach your potential, it's essential to acknowledge the beliefs that you hold about yourself, as well as your beliefs about other people and the world around you. And it's important to check in on a periodic basis to see if those beliefs still hold true and if they are limiting you in any way.

Exercise: Updating Your Belief Systems

The exercise above should give you the information that will help you think about the answers to the questions below.

Step 1: Answer the following questions:

- What core beliefs do you hold about yourself based on past experiences and events?
- How do they impact you today?
- How do these beliefs translate into behaviors?

For example, if you were told as a child that you're not creative, was it really true and does it still hold true for you? If it doesn't, have you been able to reframe your self-image as that belief has become obsolete?

I was sure when I was younger that I wasn't creative and I shied away from activities like drawing or writing stories. But I'm pretty good at coming up with new and innovative ideas at work today, so maybe that's not true about me anymore . . . or maybe it never was true. Maybe it was just an opinion.

Step 2: Share this information with a mentor, coach, family member, trusted friend, or spouse. They can provide an objective view on how accurate those beliefs are and on whether they're empowering or unnecessarily limiting for you.

Step 3: Work on changing beliefs that don't ring true anymore.

If, for example, you believe you don't speak up and aren't influential in meetings, observe yourself in meetings to see whether that's really true. Are you good at speaking up during small, informal meetings, but more reticent at bigger, more formal sessions? Are you able to provide good analytical feedback when you're asked for your input? Do you provide good agendas or other prep work that makes meetings more focused and productive?

Focusing on the ways you do make yourself heard and influence outcomes will help you to see yourself differently. And you can use that as a launching point for changing your hardwiring. If you're already more influential than you thought, then maybe it's not that big a leap to offer input before you're asked or to be more assertive in larger groups. Of course, speaking up at one meeting isn't going to change your belief. You have to behave consistently over time to completely uproot and supplant it. Start by asserting your new belief in environments that are relatively safe, say in a team meeting, rather than a meeting with the board.

Learning to Let Your Values Be Your Guide

I understand that over time, the currents of life and work can carry you off course, often so subtly that you don't realize it's happening until you notice you're somewhere far from where you wanted to be.

After spending 14 years in the corporate world, running human resource teams, I realized that I was ready to turn to the next chapter in my career. My entrepreneurial bent was pushing to the surface and I wanted to build a business that would create innovative ways to develop and advance new business leaders, something I both knew and cared about.

Just as I had done at the start of my career, before embarking on this major transition, I once again identified and prioritized my core values. This was not a laundry list of all my values about everything. I am talking about my nonnegotiables—the ones that really mattered to me. They included being in a work situation where I would have real ownership over the work I produced (for better or for worse), where I could pursue continuous learning and personal growth, and where I could create new things, take risks, build relationships, and have fun.

Seeing this list of entrepreneurial values reinforced my confidence that I was making the right career move and those values continue to make my short list today.

I think of this list as my compass—a reminder of what is important to me and of what I want to accomplish. It also helps me to choose the right direction in which to pursue my version of success. It helps to ensure that I, and not those around me, shape my dreams.

Not paying attention to your own compass can get you into trouble. It can lead to jobs that are ill fitting and unsatisfying, and it can get you stuck somewhere between the eighteenth floor (management) and the executive suite penthouse. It's incredible how often I see talented people fail to match their personal values to their career choices. For example, you might want to save lives but instead sell computers, and as a result you're perpetually frustrated with your work assignments. But if you instead choose to sell medical devices, you'll feel more personally committed to your product and your work, and believing in what you do will energize you to perform at your highest level.

Identifying Your Values

Through our WILL program, my organization offers a values clarification exercise (see Table 2-1 on page 32), which helps women explore and strengthen their leadership skills, confidence, and competence areas. The exercise usually helps women to see that when their values are aligned with their day-to-day work, they are much more energized and much less stressed. This exercise also demonstrates to them that they will be happier and better equipped to reach higher levels of success by knowing their values and designing their lives around them.

You can start to identify your values by examining your past experiences and life events. It's important to consider both your high points and low points—when you were in the groove, at your best and completely engaged in what you were doing, and conversely, when you were really hating a situation and maybe even depressed or angry about it. You can't discern your values by reflecting on situations where things were just okay. It's when situations trigger emotional responses, either positive or negative, that your values show up. Also, being aware of your triggers—when your boss, friends, or family set you off—can help you to uncover your core values. This process will tell you what motivates or inspires you, as well as what your "nonnegotiables" are.

The following exercise is an example of what I ask women to think about when I walk them through a values session in our WILL program. Try it yourself and see what you find out.

Exercise: Assessing Your Values

Step 1: Think back over several instances when you were at your best, highly fulfilled, and focused. Jot down what worked for you: the people you worked with, the goal you had to achieve, or the environment where you worked.

Step 2: Look for the themes or patterns common to these events or experiences. Consider what values they reflect, such as accomplishment orientation, risktaking, independence, creativity, and so on.

Step 3: Next, think of events or experiences that were unsatisfying and did not contribute to your growth. Again, after you have identified a few, look for the themes and patterns here. Why were you dissatisfied? What made you angry? Maybe you had no authority, there were constantly shifting priorities, there wasn't great teamwork, or you lacked a common purpose with your colleagues.

Step 4: Next, make a list of the values you took from the first part of the exercise and prioritize them based on where you are now, (their rankings will change from time to time).

Step 5: Finally, don't just identify your values for yourself, share them with others when discussing career options, work concerns, or ethical dilemmas.

Your highest values might include having strong relationships with others, seeing your family happy and fulfilled, or having autonomy or flexibility in your work. Regardless of what they are, keep in mind that it's less important to consider your top 20 values than the handful that are nonnegotiable. These are your few core values and thus your compass. They will help you to define your success and make choices. These are the ones to make transparent to yourself and others, especially during job interviews and discussions about promotions.

Values in Action

For an example of how values fit into situations, consider this hypothetical example:

Sue is considering taking a new job. It will give her a promotion she's been wanting, great visibility, and a nice salary increase. She feels flattered and excited that it's been offered to her, but as she tries to imagine herself doing it, she keeps getting a knot in her stomach. She doesn't know why because she knows that she thinks it's an amazing opportunity. She explores the job further and realizes that the knot settles in when she tries to figure out the travel it will demand—she'll be on the road 50 percent of her time. But Sue just had her second child and she's realizing that her family happiness—balancing work with being a mother—are top priorities right now, and this job, fabulous though it might be, conflicts with that. She decides that taking the offer would create more frustration, unhappiness, and stress than not taking it and asks them to keep her in mind in two or three years when she might be in a different place.

Assessing Your Life-Work Values Exercise

The following values chart (Table 2-1) will allow you to avoid running headlong into the type of conflict Sue had to wrestle with. Use it to assess your level of satisfaction with your personal and work lives. It offers some common values and examples of how they appear in personal and work situations.

With a highest rating of 10, assign a rating of your level of satisfaction to each value, dividing the score between personal and work. This exercise will help you to see how well you blend and manage your values from a whole life perspective. Why divide the score of 10? Sometimes your level of satisfaction is different when looking at both personal and work life. For example, achievement may be an important value to you. Let's say you rated this value a 7 at work but 3 personally. Knowing that you are falling short on personal achievement outside of your work and profession, you begin to think of personal milestones to increase your level of satisfaction for that value. Maybe getting involved with a community outreach board or taking a course in an area you would like to personally learn and master is just one example of how to use this tool. See where your values are in sync with your personal life but not your work life and vice versa. In places where you're happy, actively work to protect against developing an imbalance. Finally, use this exercise to prioritize and focus on your top five nonnegotiable values.

Table 2-1 *Values Chart*

Value	Personal Definition	P	W	Work Definition
Accomplishment	Reaching personal milestones; gaining respect of others; having a good standing in the community	6	4	Successfully completing projects; having a great reputation; having your work recognized; being promoted
Affiliation/ Relationships	Having a close knit family or circle of friends			Feeling part of a department or division; having "connected" relationships with coworkers; teamwork; harmony in the workplace

Value	Personal Definition	P	W	Work Definition
Creativity/Innovation	Learning about art or music, pursuing hobbies; indulging new interests/ pursuits			Openness to new ideas; risk-taking; openness to change; finding new and better ways to do something
Freedom	Independence; having the right to choose			Self-directed work; minimal supervision; flexible work arrangements
Fun	Recreation; entertainment; pleasurable activities			Positive work atmosphere; informal interactions with coworkers; enjoying your work
Helpfulness	Volunteering; supporting family and friends, making a difference in the community			Assisting coworkers; coaching and mentoring; empowering others
Integrity	Honesty; trustworthiness			Transparency; fairness; opportunity; keeping commitments
Loyalty	Devotion to family/friends; patriotism			Commitment to/from a company and boss
Passion	Romance; strong enthusiasm about a hobby, interest or a "cause"			Strong positive feelings about the work; wanting to give your best effort; totally committed to what you are doing
Personal Growth & Development	Enlightenment on a variety of life-related topics; spirituality			Gaining business experience and learning new things
Security	Personal safety; financial security			Compensation and opportunity for advancement; stability of company and position

A Vision Builds Resilience and Enables Comebacks

You've spent a lot of time thinking about your values and priorities—now you'll see why it was time well spent. A clear sense of values provides a guiding force and filtering mechanism. It helps you to draw what you want, need, and deserve, and it helps you listen to that gut instinct that tells you when a seemingly perfect opportunity isn't (like Sue in our previous example).

Moreover, with the groundwork laid, you're ready for the big-picture stuff—setting a vision for yourself.

A vision can be a hard thing to get your arms around. But most simply put, it is a force that can sustain what you desire or need to get done. It's less the nuts and bolts of what you want to accomplish (i.e., getting an executive-level job by a certain time) and more the big picture of what you want your life to be (a particular mix of intellectual, family, and spiritual pursuits, for example).

When I ask clients about their vision for themselves, I often get back a "deer-in-the-headlights" look. They don't have the faintest idea what I am talking about. I explain that having a vision for yourself is another way of having an important goal for yourself. Without a vision, we look at the past rather than to our aspirations to guide our lives.

Without exception, I have observed over the years that the people who turn out to be "thought leaders," who are respected by many and have a lasting legacy of ideas, are those who have experienced difficult times. In some cases, they lost power at some stage of their career due to changing conditions that were beyond their control. Yet they survived things like giving up the corner office, or losing an impressive title for their business card. But they eventually re-emerged as great leaders. One main reason is because they had a vision for themselves.

For example, Hillary Clinton was a woman behind the scenes for eight years while her husband was in the White House. Her first high-profile foray into policymaking—her plan for national health care—was disastrous and showed her naïveté about how things are done in Washington, as well as America's appetite for that kind of massive change. But she never lost her vision of becoming an effective leader, and now she is one of the most powerful women in the country—a successful senator who is incredibly savvy about how to frame passable legislation that accomplishes her goals.

Like her, others I know had a level of confidence within themselves and a vision of who they wanted to be that they were able to hold onto and use as a rudder to keep them on course through the turbulence.

A Vision Is a Magnet

When I left the corporate world and started my own organization, I defined and worked on articulating my vision for both my organization and myself. I found that the clearer those visions became, the more I was drawn to the people I needed to make them pan out, and those same people were drawn to me.

I have people still working with me after more than 16 years, supporting our shared mission of developing great leaders. I found this so interesting that I decided to ask these people why they came to my organization and stayed. They shared with me that it was the clarity of my vision, my passion about and belief in the work we did, and the confidence that I exuded around that vision.

Seeing, believing, being, and articulating your vision with confidence is an effective tool for influencing others and for gathering the right people around your vision. As hyperbolic as it seems, I really do feel that my vision acts as a magnet, attracting intelligent, magnificent, and endearing people who are able to bring our shared vision for my business to life.

The bottom line: A vision serves as a beacon, providing a direction and purpose to help you navigate through your work. It helps you to continue moving forward in spite of all the distractions and disappointments and detours that you encounter along the way. And there will be disappointments and distractions: mergers, acquisitions, layoffs, missed promotions, failed projects, and the like.

Why is this vision thing particularly important for women? A study conducted by Harris Interactive indicated that 4 out of 10 qualified women (37 percent) reported that they had left their work voluntarily. Having broken through the traditional glass ceiling and reaching the executive suite, many found that they were dissatisfied or questioning the direction in which they were headed. I have heard many accomplished women say that when they get to that place of power, they find themselves asking, "Is this it?" They become frustrated and find the position is not doing it for them. It doesn't bring the sense of fulfillment and happiness they had thought it would. Usually, it wasn't the level of power that disagreed with them. Rather the specific position that got them to the executive suite wasn't aligned with their personal vision and thus, it wasn't the position they could best serve.

When I coach women who are moving from an individual contributor role to a manager's job that is meant to prime them for an executive role, I ask them to step back and look outside their day-to-day activities. I ask them to describe to me how they see themselves in a broader context, in their personal life and career.

I remember one woman who had a very vivid vision for herself. She saw herself succeeding in three major roles: mother, business leader, and servant to others in the community. What that meant for her was that a big piece of her life was going to be focused outside of work, on her family, and community activities. She knew clearly what she wanted her family experience to be for each of her children and for herself. She also had a clear picture of where she wanted to take her organization and the kind of culture and work environment she wanted to build for her employees. Finally, she also was committed to making a difference for others who were less fortunate and was starting a local chapter of Habitat for Humanity. Having this vision for herself and knowing what she wanted to do in these key areas of her life helped her to choose her priorities and measure her successes.

If you don't have a clearly defined vision for yourself, consider the following questions.

Exercise: Creating Your Vision

1. Have you defined the important roles you have or want to have in your life?

2. Can you clearly articulate what success looks like in each of these roles?

3. Do you know what your priorities are around these roles you want to have? And have you established important goals, objectives, and boundaries to achieve them?

4. Describe your ideal work environment: people you'd work with, type of work you'd do, the schedule you'd keep, who your customers would be, and how you would benefit them.

5. If you had one year to live, what would you do?

6. If you were about to die, what are the three things that people would say about you? How would they say you have made a difference or impacted others in a positive way? What is something that will continue to live on because of

you? How do these answers compare to what you would want the answers to be?

All of the areas you explored in this chapter make up you as a "whole" leader. Great leadership means believing, being, and living out your role in an integrated way. It is about blending your beliefs, values, professional goals and desires, and all the other dimensions that make up work and life. It is not easy and many of us are leading in a very stressful and fast-paced environment. John Donahue, president of eBay Market Places and former worldwide managing director of Bain, stressed that it is important to maintain a sense of self no matter where you are. He warned, "The world can shape you if you let it. To have a sense of yourself as you live, you must make conscious choices. Sometimes the choices are really hard, but you make the right one in the end."

There's a saying, "If you don't know where you are going, any road will get you there." To not have a vision is to not know where you're going. You can meander, or worse, you can wind up letting someone else navigate your career according to their terms rather than your vision.

Don't wait for someone else to set a destiny for you. Life is too precious. And you have too much to give to waste it on an agenda that might not be in your best interests or fulfill your desires or be aligned with your values.

On to the Sticky Floors

This soul-searching is a great and essential warm-up exercise. Now that you've got the muscles that deal with introspection, assessment, and self-improvement in gear, you're ready to move ahead to the main part of the book, the sticky floors. Plunge ahead, or if you have a particular issue that needs dealing with, turn to page 46 for a guide to the sticky floors and head to the one from which you most need to pull free.

Sure it's daunting, but look at how much you've already accomplished. Hopefully you're already seeing an improvement in your work and in your work-life balance. So trust that you're ready and that you can do this, and that you'll be an even better person, primed for the executive suite, when you're done.

Chapter 3

Balancing Your Work and Life

Is Your Life Spinning Out of Control?

Have you ever had one of those days when you're there in the office, sitting at your desk and suddenly it occurs to you that you're surrounded by silence because everyone else has gone home?

You massage your brow and think about how stressed and burned out you've been feeling at a job that once thoroughly energized you. You realize that more and more you've been thinking of leaving. It seems like the requests and demands have kept building and building to the point where they seem chronically impossible. And your personal life? What's that?

Or maybe you've looked up in horror to see that it's 8 p.m. and you immediately realize that you've missed your daughter's "back-to-school night," or your son's Little League game, or your yoga class or . . . fill in the blank. You can't believe you've let time get away from you. How did this happen? You're a good mom, girlfriend, wife, person— although a very guilt ridden one right now. Where *are* your priorities, you can't help but think, knowing full well that the answer seems to be staring up at you from your desk.

If you're lucky, you decide at a moment like this that things are going to change because your workaholic schedule is impacting the quality of your personal life far more than you're comfortable with, and ironically, it's sapping satisfaction, energy, and focus from the job itself. The more time you spend at work, it seems, the less you like it. If you're really lucky, you'll remember your vow the next day and will make the effort needed to make those changes happen.

Take comfort in the knowledge that you are not alone. I routinely see examples of work-life imbalance when I counsel employees at organizations that are supposedly committed to being great places to work. Everyone in those organizations, but women in particular, wants to know how they can find balance in the constant juggling of work and family. They all want to know if it's really possible to get that next raise, promotion, or plum assignment without sacrificing their personal life.

The Balancing Act—Know Your Threshold!

I remember quite clearly the rough and tumble days of starting SHAMBAUGH more than 16 years ago. I was a one-person show for some time. I did the administrative work, marketing, proposal writing—oh yes, and the actual consulting work, too. At some point I made the insane decision to go back to school for a master's degree at the same time. The demands of building my business and keeping up with my classes didn't leave much time for anything else. I worked seven days a week and studied late at night, early mornings, and on weekends.

Eighteen months after opening up shop, I landed my first big contract. I hired staff for back-office support and day-to-day operations, so that I could take care of my very important client and acquire others.

I was elated about the business growing, but eventually I realized that I had to come up for air.

One Sunday morning, I came into my office, sat down at my desk, and started pulling files I wanted to work on out of a drawer—my usual routine. Suddenly I asked myself, why am I doing this? There was nothing that couldn't wait until Monday morning. I could be playing tennis or going to my favorite church service—things I once enjoyed doing on the weekend—and yet I chose to come into work.

I realized that coming into the office to stay on top of things was something I needed to do to get SHAMBAUGH up and running. But now, the business was doing very well and it didn't need that all-out effort from me. At some point, I began coming in on the weekends for the sake of coming in. I was on autopilot, and in a bit of a rut. I couldn't recall having a personal life, so I knew I must have been sabotaging it. Sitting at the desk and thinking it all through, I realized that working for the sake of working probably wasn't good for me. And if it wasn't good for me, it probably wasn't good for the business that relied on me either.

It was time for me to reprioritize and channel some time back into the things in my personal life that I valued. I scheduled in time for my Sunday morning church service and called up my tennis friends to get back on their roster. And when family or friends asked me to take a trip with them, I went—reclaiming an enjoyable thing that I had given up for some time.

I learned from that experience that it is important to step back periodically and checkin on yourself. How are you conducting your life, where is your time and effort taking you, and does it make sense? There are times when we need to put an all-out effort into our job or career or personal development, or our family, such as that period when I was trying to start my company. But when it crosses the line from being an episode in your life to being your everyday norm, that's when life swings out of balance.

Avoiding imbalance and burnout is another way of keeping our eye on the big picture, pacing ourselves, and making sure we're putting our efforts into the right things at the right time for the right reasons.

Do you want to know whether you're working for a purpose or working for the sake of working? Answer these questions:

- What have some of your past goals been?
- How did you know when you had achieved them?
- Did you take time out to revel in them? Or to at least do something to congratulate yourself and signify the accomplishment?
- If not, why not? Were you afraid of slowing down? Had it been so long since you'd taken time for yourself that you didn't know how to? Did it never occur to you that you might need a break?

Kicking a habit is hard and work can become a habit. If you have an inkling that it's time for you to move into a new work habit, but you aren't sure how to begin, think about these questions:

- Lately, have you felt like you're hitting a wall, or that you're just flat-out tired?
- What are the triggers that make you feel you are in conflict with yourself?
- What behaviors or subconscious patterns are the ones that are not working for you anymore?
- What new behaviors would you like to use to replace those that no longer work?
- What new boundaries and expectations do you need to set with yourself and with others?
- What can you do today, tomorrow, and next week to start moving in the right direction?

The Facts About Work-Life Balance

Since the 1980s, work-life balance has become an increasingly talked about issue. I remember starting my career in the late 70s and early 80s. Even with so much to prove as a woman in a male-dominated industry, I "left work at work" for the most part. I might bring home some things to read or make a few phone calls from home, but it was much easier to separate work from personal time without PDAs, e-mails, and cell phones to create a permanent link. The belief that all work is 24/7 and global, as well as the ubiquity of home offices, make us feel that we can, and therefore probably should, always be at work.

Studies have shown that living a balanced life fosters the resilience we need to be successful leaders. The highly successful executives I coach and work around overwhelmingly have well-rounded lives. They work hard at their jobs but also find time for family and friends and make it a priority to take care of themselves. It shows in their ability to approach day-to-day challenges and problems with focus, energy, grounded perspective, and good judgment.

Maintaining that sense of balance is important to both women and men, and a challenge to everyone. But women, by virtue of our wiring or our situations, or both, feel it more. In a recent survey, 83 percent of women with jobs agreed that they have a hard time balancing work and family, and say they are trying to find a better rhythm in their life. That's no surprise because women are under more pressure than men in most cases to fulfill and balance all the multi-roles in their life. Another driving factor, which we will talk more about later in the chapter, is the need to please and setting higher than expected standards for ourselves.

All organizations go through periods where employees are stretched very thin and some organizations or bosses accept long hours as the norm for the wrong reasons. But I try to help my clients see that more often than not, women unknowingly bring this work-life crisis on themselves.

It's their sticky floor.

Now, I am not here to say that men aren't capable of having bad priorities. They were mastering workaholism long before we were allowed out of the steno pool. But women have natural traits and virtues that can work to their disadvantage when it comes to managing work and life.

If I were a doctor, I would look for symptoms of work-life imbalance. I would ask: Do you . . .

- Feel caught in an exhausting cycle of projects or demands that seem endless?
- Feel angry at people who ask you for favors, even reasonable ones?
- Have a difficult time saying *no* to others even when you want to?
- Feel burned out?
- Feel you've lost your creative spark?
- Feel you've lost your self-motivation?

If you have any or all of these symptoms, you'll need to look for the root cause of your problem. A chronic lack of work-life balance can be the result of your reluctance to delegate, extremely high standards, a skewed sense of loyalty, or a refusal to set boundaries. You can almost think of these things as the virus underlying the symptoms. For a deeper diagnosis, consider whether any of the following tendencies for women strike a chord with you.

The Multitasking Syndrome: Many women are wired to be good multi-taskers, but it backfires when they overtask. They take on too many projects or goals, and wind up juggling too much.

Inevitably, they lose sight of priorities and fail to make progress on the things that are most important to them. As a result, they feel frustrated and in conflict with their own priorities, and burnout usually isn't far behind.

The Martyr Syndrome: Many women are devoted wives and mothers, and fiercely loyal employees. They will go the extra mile to support, fix, or make things better for others. They feel guilt when they aren't there for one of these constituents the way they think they ought to be. But they also resent not having the time they would like for themselves. They forget to establish a broad vision of life for themselves and wind up burning the candle at both ends. Again, what is the result? They wind up demoralized and exhausted and yes, burnout lurks ahead for them as well.

The Self-Critic Syndrome: Some women turn introspection and self-examination into a never-ending cycle of self-criticism. They over-analyze their potential flaws as well as their accomplishments, and as a result, they never feel they're good enough. They obsess and overwork to compensate and wind up working to keep up and prove themselves, rather than to get ahead. The result? They never learn to play to their natural strengths and never feel fulfilled. They can be burnt out and deny that it's okay to do something about it.

The Perfectionist Syndrome: Some women need to bring even the smallest details to their level of perfection and, as a result, are reluctant to hand off work to others or to delegate. They become the barrier to getting things done rather than the efficient achiever they believe themselves to be. Worse, they come to be seen as worker bees rather than leaders. The result? They wonder why they keep getting passed over for promotions, and become demoralized and resentful that their hard work isn't being recognized.

To Live a Balanced Life You Need a Life Plan

When I talk to audiences about this topic, I reinforce the fact that having a balance in your work and life is like planning a drive to some distant destination. You need a roadmap so that you know where you're going and how you plan to get there. It can be brutal to initially develop your "life map," but if you don't someone else will.

Planning out this life map is just another way to help yourself understand what goals you want to accomplish in a given timeframe, maybe a year. But you probably want to think further out and pose the harder, "big picture" questions to yourself: What do you want to accomplish over the course of your life? Do you want to have a marriage? Do you want to have children? Do you have financial goals? Do you maintain your health so you can do the things you enjoy and have the energy and stamina to be a leader in today's ever changing and demanding world?

This is difficult, especially when the answers to these questions are not entirely within our control. But cultivating this self-awareness provides the focus and courage you need to make an investment in yourself.

In my conversations with women, I encourage them to believe and to act on the idea that at the end of the day, they really are in control of their work-life balance.

You do have choices regarding how you live your life, yet these choices can sometimes be difficult choices. Husbands and children are important; friends and aging parents are important; your personal well-being and sense of achievement are important. The conflict among these various parts of our lives can come to a head just when we are ready to reach for those prime executive-level jobs. This often happens at a stage in our lives where we have both teenagers and older parents needing our attention and care.

I've noticed that people who have successful work-life balance have a formula that works for them. They are good at organizing and prioritizing the things that are essential for their personal and professional well-being. Once they make a decision about the right place to be at any given time, they don't second-guess themselves. They know they might not always get it right, but take it on faith that they make the best decisions they can at any given time and then move forward to the next decision.

Two Women Who Had a Plan and Lived the Plan!

Nancy Schumann and Sandy Sullivan are leading the pack in job sharing at General Electric (GE). They share the job of Program Manager for Diversity and Inclusive Leadership. Nancy and Sandy agreed that by stepping back and taking time to organize and prioritize their whole life dimensions, and then putting a plan together to manage those priorities, gave them the opportunity to have full personal lives while also retaining the opportunity to be very successful in their leadership roles at GE.

Sandy works Monday, Tuesday, and Friday. Nancy works Tuesday, Wednesday, and Thursday. "We make it work professionally and personally together," says Nancy. Nancy has four children with a husband who travels extensively for his job. Sandy is a single mother of two.

The two women observe that women sometimes fall short in attaining a fulfilling career by assuming that their organization knows what they want. "No one will come to you with a silver platter," Sandy said. "You can't assume that they know what you want. You have to have the confidence and courage to know what you want and make the appropriate request."

Sandy observes, "We are all running so fast, doing so much, and trying to be so many things to so many people. Some women wake up one day feeling frustrated and they don't really know what they want anymore." They say that in some ways it is the superwoman image that got us where we are, trying to do everything on our own and to be the very best in our abilities all the time that causes this dilemma.

The traditional corporate formula for success has been based on the assumptions of what the company wants. To some extent, that approach has been wired in our heads. We believe that this is how things work and that it constitutes the formula for success. But, Sandy advises that it doesn't have to be that way; today the workplace is a two-way street where the employee is equally responsible for thinking about and suggesting different career paths. "Don't wait for the company to come to you and provide what they may not know you want. They are supporting your growth and opportunities, but they can't read your mind."

Sandy and Nancy say that women who are successful in managing both their personal and professional lives possess the following:

1. Self-awareness: They've come to the realization that at some point they were totally overwhelmed. Once you can say that, hear it, and own it, then the time is right to make a change and do something about it.

2. Humility: These women know they don't have all the answers. They're willing to reach out to a coach or mentor. They are not afraid to talk about their situation or concerns —they realize that it does not make you seem incompetent or imply that you are not a team player, or suggest that you should be passed over for the next promotion.

3. Realistic expectations: They realize that women who stay on the fast track will probably get more stock options and

other perks as they progress faster through their careers, and they are okay with that trade-off. They are willing to take the ebb and flow.

4. Diverse interests: They have to have multiple dimensions to their lives and understand that this is one of the positive trade-offs. Nancy is active with the Girl Scouts and other community activities and ran a marathon at age 40.

5. Leadership: These women are calm and self-possessed. They know how to inspire and delegate, yet they don't allow themselves to get caught on that frantic treadmill of overwork.

And the bottom line is that these women are comfortable with who they are and know what they want!

The Wheel of Life

Women in our Women in Leadership and Learning (WILL) program do an activity called the Wheel of Life that helps them to create a work-life plan. Many of the participants find this exercise fascinating because it's the first time they've taken the time to think about their life holistically and reflect on the dimensions that are most important to them. They also get to reflect on how well they are "living up to" the ideals they have for themselves.

Needless to say, most of the women in our training programs are very successful business leaders, and it's not unusual for us to hear that a great deal of their energy and effort over the past few years has been focused on their work. But it's the "Wheel of Life" and not the "Wheel of Work" (which would be much more comfortable for many women!). These women do know, on some level, that they have other things they still need to fit in alongside work. The wheel helps them to literally see what's most important to them now, laid out right in front of them.

Once women see the slices they want to have in their pie, they can see how big those different slices are and how close that comes to how big or small they would like each one to be. From there it's easier for them to set some specific work-life goals and near-term priorities.

Following is an example of the Wheel of Life.

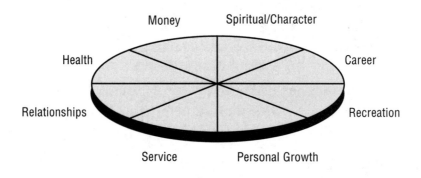

The following are definitions for each spoke of the wheel of life.

Personal growth means the same thing to everyone but manifests itself differently from one person to another. It might mean becoming a better mother, or getting your MBA, or learning to play golf. Think about what it means to you. What is the new thing you most want to learn to do or interest you would like to develop?

Money is usually a dollar figure you want to earn or it could be a long-term financial goal and long-term security. But it can also encompass benefits, job security, or opportunities for advancement.

Relationships include family and friends as well as colleagues and clients. What constitutes a relationship for you? Who are your most important relationships and what kinds of things do you want to do with those folks? Do you get as much time as you would like or think you should have for those activities?

Health has to do with your mental, emotional, and physical well-being. We're more aware than ever of the need to exercise and stay fit, but what about the other aspects of health? Do you exercise? Do you get enough sleep? Do you eat right on most days and keep your vices (chocolate, wine, French fries) to a moderate level? Are health issues, lack of energy, or insomnia impacting other aspects of your life?

Spiritual/character refers to that connection you have with something greater than yourself. It might be religion, a philosophy, or some other system that provides you with guidance and inner strength. What do you believe in? Is it important to you today? If so, why and how does it manifest in your everyday life?

Career is more than just your job. It's the broader areas of interest, dreams, and passions that are related to what you do for a living. It's the big picture and small details that make your workday meaningful. How does your current job relate to your career aspirations?

The components will change over time. When you make your wheel, feel free to take out any component that's not important to you now and insert another that is—and revisit when you believe it might have changed.

I encourage you to take a few moments now and chart your wheel right here in the book as it is today.

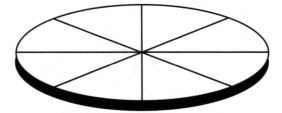

Your Ideal Wheel of Life.

Now, create the wheel you would like to have. Step back and think about some of the core dimensions of your life—what are the non-negotiables or things that matter to you? Take a moment to begin charting out how you would like those to be one or two years from now. For example, you may want to focus more on your own health, so going to the gym twice a week or working with a trainer once a week is a start. Once you charted your wheel, on a scale from 1 to 10, rate your level of satisfaction in each area, as shown below.

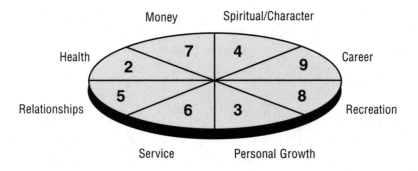

Don't worry if your wheel is short on 10s. Few wheels reflect lives as perfectly well rounded as we like (no wonder the road of life is so bumpy!).

The shape of the wheel doesn't really matter because it will change. The power of the wheel comes in the questions you can ask yourself once you've completed it. Try to answer as honestly as you can.

Now Questions

- What does your wheel look like today?
- Are you living your life in a way that is aligned with your values and priorities?
- Are you paying attention to the parts of your life that are most important to you?
- What parts are being slighted? Do you want to do anything about that? What might you do and what's a reasonable timeframe for getting started?
- If you want to make some changes to better address some aspect of your life, what will you need to do? Or, what will you need to stop doing?

Future Questions

- What do you want your wheel to look like two or three years from now?
- What are the obstacles you'll face in getting it to look like that?
- What opportunities can you take advantage of to build toward that future wheel?

Don't forget to keep those promises to yourself! When you feel yourself sliding back into those easy habits that will push your life out of balance again, use this wonderful tool to get yourself back on track. For an extra bit of motivation, remember, "This is not a dress rehearsal!"

Five Keys to Work-Life Balance

Another valuable way to sort your priorities and examine your life is to make a list (on paper) of the many roles you play and determine what success looks like to you in regard to those roles.

We all have a myriad of roles we play in life. We have our title and an image of who we are at work. In our personal lives, we might also be mothers, daughters, wives, girlfriends, lovers, sisters, and friends. These roles define who we are in relation to people who are most important to us. Each role can be a tremendous source of joy as well as a significant drain on our time and attention.

Then there are the roles we play in our greater community: neighbor, caregiver, volunteer, community leader, a member of organizations or a spiritual community. These provide fulfilling opportunities to make a contribution beyond our jobs and our close circle of family and friends. They can also be a source of guilt when we are unable to participate in public life as much as we think we should.

For most of us, there aren't enough hours in the day to be successful in each of these realms—personal, professional, and communal —all of the time. Unless we prioritize and say *no*, we can be busy every minute of every day and not feel that we've accomplished anything when we crawl into bed exhausted.

How do we define success in these broad roles? In their book, *Just Enough*, Laura Nash and Howard Stevenson examine what business leaders concur are the four essential elements of lasting and worthwhile success. I find this premise useful because it provides a simple way to look at goal setting in relation to these public and private spheres of our lives.

The four elements are:

- **Happiness:** having feelings of pleasure or contentment about your life

- **Achievement:** having accomplishments you are proud of
- **Significance:** having a positive impact on people who matter to you
- **Legacy:** passing along your values or ways of doing things in ways that help others find future success

If the authors are correct and these four categories are what we are trying to achieve to feel successful in our lives, then we can use them as a measuring stick as we make choices about what we want to accomplish, both short and long term in these various roles of ours. What do you want to accomplish in your personal, professional, and community life and how will those goals get you closer to bringing these four elements to each of those spheres?

Whether you follow this concept as a guide or set goals for yourself in a different set of categories (such as the Wheel of Life), I think the key is to prioritize and focus on no more than four or five goals that matter the most to you and use them to determine how you spend your discretionary time and how you measure your success at the end of each day.

Another important consideration—to bring reality back into the picture—is that you will, from time to time, find yourself in specific situations that usurp your time and attention and temporarily take you away from this more holistic approach to your life. Those situations might include having small children, caring for an aging or ill parent, starting a new job, moving, divorce, or supporting your partner through an important event in his or her life. But that's okay. It's all right to take detours once in a while! But, take them consciously and with intention and check back in periodically to make sure you eventually get back into a groove that will restore that balance you've been working on.

Anita Phillips, now CFO of Carlson Marketing International in Plymouth, Minnesota, recalls narrowly getting off track, and back on again early in her career, when she was working her way up through the ranks at Arthur Andersen. In a work culture that was known at the time for being difficult for women, she managed to win a promotion to the next level of senior leadership, the crucial stepping-stone to becoming a partner. She expected to make adjustments, learn new things, and work hard to come up to speed in this important new high-profile role. But a year into the job, something wasn't right.

"For the first time, I wasn't enjoying my job," she says. She realized that as a rank-and-file accountant she had been used to her work having an ebb and flow. "There would be the busy season where you would have no life, but at some point, things would slow down." Since becoming a manager, she seemed to be in one unending busy season and she was getting tired of always being at the office.

She says this sudden and acute dissatisfaction made her begin to understand that she wasn't going about her job the right way and had to rethink it. She realized that as a manager she needed to make better use of her staff, to delegate and reorder her priorities so that she would be able to both excel in her new role and go home at night on a regular basis. Anita said, "I knew something had to change. And this pushed me to realize that I could not do my direct reports' jobs for them. I went about setting new expectations for them in terms of my role and made a conscious decision to delegate and do more coaching and mentoring."

In other words, she consciously made the transition from staff to manager and gained better work-life balance in the process.

Get Focused!

There's a good reason why so many of us set New Year's resolutions! We need a starting point for setting and working toward a desired goal—an excuse for a fresh start. For years my resolution was always to slow down, work less, and play more. For my best friend, it was always to lose weight and exercise regularly. No matter what you think your resolution should be this year and no matter how many days are left until December 31, never mind.

Trust me, any day can be the day you give yourself a fresh start. You can renew your focus and set a resolution on any day of the year, and the very best day is probably TODAY!

You know what your goals are in the various parts of your life. And you've set priorities to help you give each of them adequate attention. Now comes the hard part: living your life accordingly, despite the many people and forces that are oblivious to your new agenda.

One of the methods I use with the women I coach is to have them look at and work on their time budget. If you want to save more or spend differently, the first thing a financial planner does is ask you to look at what you spend your money on, so you can see where you already have more of a cushion than you thought, and where you need to cut back and reallocate your spending to optimize your budget. Try the same approach with the hours in your day. Looking at how you spend your time each day will show you places where you can buy some time before you begin to reallocate your attention.

A simple hourly log will do just fine. Note every hour of your day at work and home for two weeks. You'll become acutely aware of all you do and can begin to sort your time into "musts, shoulds, and coulds." Cutting out the *coulds* in one sphere of your life will give you the time you want for the *musts* in the other spheres. For example, sending an employee to represent you at a weekly late-afternoon meeting that you like to attend, but aren't required to, will give you that hour to have dinner at home with your partner, drive the soccer team to a game, or rejoin your girlfriends for their weekly gabfest. Maybe limiting your volunteer commitments from four hours a week to two will give you the time you are looking for to go to a yoga class or to grocery shop and stock up on healthier meals.

Create a new time "budget" that reflects your new priorities and time allotments. Take it to work and read it twice a day. Bring it home and put it back on your night table so it's there to refer to first thing in the morning. Do this for three months. Eventually the process will become intuitive and you'll carry what you need in your head rather than having to refer to it on paper.

Establish Your Boundaries and Communicate Them

Remember that *you* are the one making changes in how you prioritize and order your life. Everyone around you is still the same. The office workaholics will still try to call 5:00 meetings, the chatty clients will still call when you're on a deadline, and that woman at church or temple will still pressure you into giving more time than you'd like to your volunteer commitments.

The good news is that effective change starts at the top. The higher up you climb, the better the position you're in to not only set expectations around how you work, but also influence the tone and work-life culture for your team or division, or even your whole company.

Sharon Allen, Chairman of Deloitte & Touche USA, and listed among the world's most powerful women in *Forbes*, says this: "If you want to balance work and life, it's important to be transparent about your goals and expectations. We need to be clear about letting others know we are leaving work at 5 p.m. to see our son's soccer game. And as executives, we need to be seen doing these things to let others know it is okay to leave at 5:00 for their son's soccer game. This sets a healthy expectation of what's accepted for yourself and for others."

All you can do is acknowledge that you always have choices and you can always say *no*. You can go to that meeting or tell the person you have a prior commitment and leave. You can take that call now or return it when it's more convenient for you. You can run the church book fair again or stand firm that you can only help someone else run it this year. If you are tempted to say *yes*, out of habit or a reluctance to disappoint others, first remind yourself that you are *choosing* to make this impromptu change and as a result, something else on your schedule will have to go. Decide what that thing would be and then agree that *just for today* you'll let it go, or tell yourself that you don't want to let it go and offer up the *no* that you don't like to give, but know you need to.

A Word About *NO*

For some of us, *no* is very difficult. We want to see ourselves and be seen as the can-do person, or we want to help out and save the day, or we don't like to disappoint. If saying *no* is too difficult for you, maybe you need a little coaching—think of it as helping to build your *no* muscle. There are books and seminars on assertiveness and any executive coach can help with this.

Know that you can say no by saying yes. I have done that when I feel swamped and really want to help out or support someone's request. I may get a call to sit on an advisory board or sit on a committee that I believe in. While I know in my heart this will take time I don't have at the moment, I will say that I would be happy to help you, but can't do it right now. I just need to finish up some top priorities and then check back with me. And if you still can't, then think about whether you can offer the name of someone you know who might have the time and who also would enjoy it or see an opportunity for themselves in terms of exposure or their own career development.

One of the participants in our leadership program for women gave me the best *no* I've ever heard. It goes like this: "Sorry. Love to. Can't." And actually, you can use those three responses in any order. Try it and have some fun saying *no*!

Build Your Support Network and Actually Use It

We look at strategic networking from a work/career perspective in a later chapter, but now I want to address what I have recently heard referred to as your lifeline or life support group. As professional women and high achievers, too often we feel we have to go it alone to do something well and get credit for it. In some situations that's true, but it's definitely not true when it comes to work-life balance issues. In this sphere, we need people to fill in our gaps, make up for our shortcomings, and provide the emotional, moral, and practical support we need to stay energized enough to keep our priorities straight and keep ourselves in balance (or to get back on track when that balance slips out of our grasp).

Think of it this way: As human beings we run on energy. Occasionally our tank is drained and we need to fill it up again before we can keep going. Our family and friends are the source of that "refueling" process.

For me, my sister, Cindy is always willing to listen with her heart and hear the struggle beneath my words when I have a personal dilemma. I always have my assistant block my calendar twice a year for me to spend time out at my favorite retreat, Telluride, Colorado. The energy of the mountains, skiing, and beautiful views and vistas I take in while hiking help me to recharge and maintain a healthy perspective on the things that matter most. This has been a wonderful time to connect with my family and good friends in a calm and beautiful part of the world and avoid the distractions that everyday life presents back at the office. I also have a colleague who makes me laugh when I feel totally frustrated with a work situation. Together they provide me with the emotional energy I need. I turn to others to provide me with new insights into work situations and guidance on particular projects. These are my mentors and coaches. Finally, I have a small board of directors who provide me with guidance on how to sustain and grow my business. In different ways, all these folks help me work through my work-life issues and succeed at the things that are most important in my personal and work lives.

Think for a minute about the people who constitute your "lifeline" and think about how they might help you in the next week as you begin to rebalance your life and work. It's important to remember that you have others you can call on for specific help or for moral support. Reach out to them and let them contribute to your success! And do the same for others who reach out to you.

In fact, that's the one thing I think is okay to do even if it's not on your weekly "to-do" list—help someone spontaneously and consider it your repayment to those who have helped you along the way!

Start Now and Don't Worry About Being Perfect!

What, you can't start today? Why not? Too late at night to think about it? Too many other things to get done? Come on, the only excuse I think is acceptable is that you're sitting on a beach reading this book and there's no one in sight to loan you a piece of paper and a pen!

Really, go back to step 1 and get started! At the very least, you can figure out the four or five things that matter most to you this week (at work and in life) and write down what you need to do in the next seven days to make them happen. (And please note, a week can begin on any day; let's not wait until Monday!)

You can also get started with your time log. See what you notice and be prepared to make some hard choices. My good friend used to always say, "Fake it until you make it!" If you miss an hour on your time log—fill it in as best you remember. The time log is a tool, a means to an end, and not something you'll be graded on! See what it has to show you at the end of the week, decide what changes to make in how you're spending your time. Eventually, your time log will begin to reflect the change in your life and pretty soon, getting it "right" will become easier because you will create a "habit" of focusing on what's most important to you.

But keep in mind that changing your work-life balance is like starting a new diet. You'll fall back into old habits and you'll have a day when you don't accomplish one thing that's really important to you. Be accountable to yourself, but also forgiving. Tomorrow is always another day.

And last but not least, when you see progress and feel yourself finding that balance, don't forget to celebrate small successes along with the big ones!

Chapter 4

Embracing Good Enough

"Good, better, best . . . Never let it rest . . . Until
your good is better . . . And your better is best!"

HARD AS IT might be to imagine, that school cheer captures in very simple terms what I will be talking about in this chapter. It's just a little rhyming ditty and very easy to remember. I remember it because someone wrote it in my autograph book in fourth grade, and it was probably written in yours as well. Little did those young scribblers know they were inspiring a sticky floor for those women who are prone to be overachievers!

Here's an example of how this sticky floor—ceaseless perfectionism—manifests itself in the office:

Bob, Sarah's manager, was expecting a report from her on Thursday. On Friday afternoon he didn't have it yet, and when he asked her about it, she said she was going to work on it over the weekend. Bob was dumbfounded. He asked her politely, but with a bit of an edge in his voice, what the holdup was. Sarah said she just wanted to rework the charts and rewrite some of the work her team had given her before he saw it. Bob's response was, "But I just asked for a draft!"

Sarah's explanation: "Even a draft represents me and I need to be sure it is right." This made a lot of sense to Sarah but Bob went away wondering if she would ever give up dealing with the details and micromanaging her people. Worse, he also wondered how, if she couldn't do a simple draft report for the executive committee, he could ever consider her for a position on that committee. "She would drive herself—and everyone else—crazy," he decided.

The Perfectionism Syndrome—When a Virtue Becomes an Obstacle

Perfectionism can be a virtue—an Olympic athlete can't settle for anything short of it—but in the workplace it can be a big sticky floor. If it becomes a manager's dominant trait it can push aside other priorities and values and actually keep talented women out of the executive suite. In Sarah's case, she was so engrossed in her self-imposed need to be perfect that she lost sight of other important things, like meeting deadlines, acknowledging and responding to her boss's sense of urgency, and trusting the work of the people she delegated to. This example better defines perfectionism, which is the propensity for setting extremely high standards and being displeased with anything less.

Perfectionists function in a mode where nothing is ever good enough. But their self-imposed standards are far higher than what others expect or even need. This trait becomes apparent to others when a manager rewrites every report multiple times, redoes her team's work every time, and needs to respond to everything personally because everything is important. The question for Sarah and other perfectionists is: When is good, good enough? And when is getting the right work done, in the right way, through the right people more important than being personally flawless?

Know What Is Good Enough

Elizabeth Lewis, a partner at Cooley Godward, recalls giving up on perfection and finding balance instead when she was a young attorney juggling a demanding litigation practice with a family and a high-powered social life.

She and her husband belonged to a dinner club where each couple took a turn hosting a dinner party. "Everyone kept upping the ante and there was pressure to fix the best meal yet," she says. When her turn came, she found herself after a long day of work, standing in her kitchen figuring out how to make Oysters Rockefeller with her toddler children pulling on her skirt, trying to get her attention.

"I realized I didn't like this sense of conflict I felt inside me. I wanted to give my kids the attention they were asking for. I didn't like being a gourmet cook and didn't want to do it," she says. "It dawned on me that I could just make lasagna and a salad and dinner would be fine."

She continues, "It was a really shaping and memorable moment because it was the point when I gave myself permission to not excel in everything."

Everyone has situations where the work needs to be examined down to the finest level of detail and checked "one more time" for accuracy. These are the situations where you can't afford to have a mistake. However, as you rise up the ladder of leadership, you have to be able to very quickly determine whether a situation requires perfection, or whether good enough will do because it's all that the situation warrants and other things are more important.

When I listen to women talk about their frustrations of getting passed over for a promotion to the higher levels of leadership, I often have to tell them that they might be stalled because of this need to be perfect. It can be hard for them to understand and accept because, ironically, that same trait has probably played a role in getting them where they are. My answer is that situations change and sometimes our greatest strength in one context can become our greatest obstacle in another.

Women who have been rewarded for working hard and "getting it done right" look at me like I'm out of my mind. But, in fact, senior business leaders use a different set of skills than middle managers. If you are overly involved, controlling, mired in the details, and hypercritical then you can't keep your eye on the big picture—and the role of a senior executive is to look after the big picture, not the minutia.

If you can't make the transition, the message you'll send is that you're a great middle manager, but not leadership material.

When taking on the CEO role for my company in the early 1990s, I learned right away that if I wanted to operate at the highest standards, which is essential for any consulting firm, I could not do all the work or manage all the pieces of the business myself.

As we grew from 10 to 15 to 20 customers, I had to figure out how to prioritize what we needed to do immediately and what could wait a few days. And I needed rules for determining which jobs I had to do personally and which could be delegated to a staff that was also growing. I know from this experience that it's hard to shake a habit that you've been acknowledged for all of your life! However, reorganizing and committing to a new way of operating was essential for me to grow the business and, frankly, not drive myself to burnout.

What also motivated me to make a change was the fact that I had seen several brilliant entrepreneurs start companies. Some succeeded by hiring good people and handing tasks off to them while others got caught up in the churn and tactical activities, and ultimately fell short of realizing optimum growth and success for their company and themselves. I did not want to be in the latter category.

Let me be candid, it wasn't easy to shift my assumptions and behaviors regarding what I worked on, how I worked, and how I valued my time. But as my company hit another growth spurt, I began to step back and identify my key business goals. Then I weighed the tasks I was doing against other tasks I could have been working on. The deciding factor in this exercise was simple; if I couldn't tie a task directly to the organization's core growth goals, I delegated it to one of several work buckets and transitioned it to my team. One of these buckets covered day-to-day work that involved administrative details, basic paperwork, and loose ends like proofing PowerPoint presentations and letters.

It seems obvious but it was amazing how much I learned from this process. Primarily, once I stopped doing them, I saw the large amount of time I had been spending on workday details. I also saw how lucky I was to have a very competent team that was actually much better than I was at those tasks. I had to accept that the memos and the emails would not be written the exact way I would have written them, and my PowerPoint slides would not have my preferred graphics and clip art. I learned that was okay because these were things where "good enough" was fine. We executed off that standard and saved perfect for when it really mattered.

The Root of Perfectionism

So, where does this perfectionist trait come from? Some will say that certain people are born with a predisposition for it. Others will say we're socialized for it. I believe that for many women it came to the forefront in school. Nothing would do except straight As and being the best in everything they did. In at least a small way, it was a response to the demands of teachers, coaches, and parents who had high expectations and who praised and rewarded and held out as good examples the students who met their high standards.

Girls, more than boys, are often raised to be people pleasers. So it's natural for the inner achiever and the inner people-pleaser to conspire to convince some girls that perfect is what they need to be—it's the thing that gets reliable results.

If you doubt that this perfectionist behavior could be reinforced simply by your being a girl, think back. Who doesn't remember checking to be sure their makeup was just right every time they walked out the door?

So, it's no wonder that the need for acceptance and recognition at work plays out in some women as striving for perfection. These high-achievers strive into the wee hours of the night to get that PowerPoint presentation just right or rerun the numbers in a report ad nauseam because they're still trying to get to the head of the class.

A Case Study of Perfectionism and Mistaken Perceptions

One of our Fortune 500 clients provides a great example of how the perfectionism issue can play out for talented managers.

The CEO hired us to address several concerns that had come to his attention about the company's pool of women leaders. The company was losing talent. Highly valued women across the company were leaving. Additionally, the company seemed unable to promote women to higher levels of leadership at the desired rate. And then the women leaders with the most potential did not want the promotion opportunities offered to them.

My team began to work with this organization and their top 150 women. We conducted a number of focus groups and extensive interviews. We found that there were organizational impediments and assumptions that contributed to the concerns regarding the retention and promotion rates, but we also found that the women had a lot of self-imposed assumptions, traits, and behaviors that were clearly impacting their ability to stay at the company, win promotion offers, and take them.

SHAMBAUGH designed a series of learning forums and targeted coaching sessions that took place over four months. During one of the early sessions, I was listening to the women talk about the challenges of having work-life balance and of meeting all the demands placed on them. Over and over again they said that they felt they could not afford to make any mistakes in their work, that they frequently doubted themselves, and that they felt they had to be better than everyone else to get ahead.

In response to that, we asked them to identify their day-to-day activities and the key objectives they were working on. We also asked them to identify the top three goals for which their managers were holding them accountable. Finally, we asked them to identify the level of performance (perfect, excellent, or it didn't matter) that they believed each activity required. Overall, the women felt that 80 percent of their work needed to be done perfectly and the remaining 20 percent needed to be excellent. And overwhelmingly, they felt that every task and activity was very important.

My initial reaction: No wonder these women feel burnt out!

We asked the women why they felt they had to work at such a high level all the time. They said they just assumed it needed to be perfect and it came out that no one had ever told them so. This was eye-opening for the women.

The lesson here is that actual evidence is as important as perceptions. We coached the women toward letting go of the pressure to be perfect and recalibrating their work standards. They acknowledged that for some work activities "good enough" would be okay.

We followed up eight months after the program and the women said that shifting their expectations had freed up time for them to be more strategic and to have better work-life balance. They also had less anxiety and stress. As a result, many of them were seeking out promotions they'd been reluctant to pursue previously and were advancing to the next levels of leadership.

In effect they turned their focus outward and began responding to the work standards conveyed by their stakeholders, instead of being driven by what they expected from themselves. That's leadership.

Signs of Being a Perfectionist

Now that I've explained what it means to be a perfectionist, where the trait comes from, and how it can play out in organizations, let's look at some different kinds of perfectionist behavior.

As is the case with so many habits—good and bad—it can be hard to recognize perfectionism without some activity, event, or advice that enables you to step back and see your patterns from the outside. The short quiz that follows might be the nudge you need.

Take a moment and check off the traits and behaviors you see in yourself:

_____ Self-doubt. You second-guess your decisions, always seek additional input to be sure, or wish you had done it differently the minute you hand off something.

_____ Perpetual dissatisfaction. The work you do and the work that others do for you is never really good enough.

_____ Superiority, or, thinking that no one will do the job as well as you will. It's impossible to delegate because when you do, you always need to review and fix the other person's work.

_____ Risk-aversion. If you go beyond your comfort zone, you might not be able to maintain your standards for yourself.

_____ A low tolerance for mistakes in yourself and others.

_____ A fear of failure.

_____ A strong need to please others.

_____ The illusion of self-imposed standards. You assume that
        your standards are what everyone else will hold you to.

You might feel that by always setting standards that are higher
than everyone else's, and succeeding in meeting them, you're achieving great things. But if it creates a fear of failure, makes you risk-
averse, and doesn't allow for any mistakes, ever . . . well, that's
limiting. The old saying, nothing ventured, nothing gained, is especially true in business. You need to be able to take measured risks and
put yourself out on a limb once in a while to grow and draw the
attention of your company's top decision makers.

In addition, perfection can be a form of tunnel vision and that can
backfire on you, too. As the anecdote about Sarah showed, no one
wants someone on their team, either above or below them, who isn't
responsive to their colleagues' needs and priorities. In addition, no
one wants to work for a boss who doesn't trust them, doesn't give
them real responsibility, always has to quiz them and "fix" their
work, and who doesn't tolerate mistakes. Another word for perfectionist is micro-manager. These bosses have trouble maintaining staff,
managing morale, and keeping productivity where it should be, and
higher-ups notice that and only let these people rise so far.

Micromanager Traits

We've already looked at some of the ways that micro-managing can
become an obstacle for advancement.

If you remain mired in the details of the work others are doing,
you won't be recognized as a strategic thinker or collaborative leader,

two core competencies required for the executive suite. You'll be seen as a good "tactical" person, which means you're acknowledged as a good manager and good executer, but probably not ready to play at the top of the organization where they need big picture people who can think strategically and innovate.

But beyond that, if you are a person who never delegates because you don't trust your team or you are a "hands on" manager, it might look like you are not developing your people or you have a leadership issue. Think about it: If you're doing the work that clearly should be the responsibility of people beneath you, your bosses could easily assume that you're making up for their slack and wonder why you need to do that. Are you not hiring the right people? Are you not cultivating them by making sure they get the training, mentoring, and experience they need to do their jobs well? Do you simply not know how to get good work out of them? Your executive team will also wonder how effectively you are grooming others to step up to their potential and eventually replace you (when you get that next big promotion).

On the other hand, if they know your people are capable, then they can assume you have a control issue. You can create the perception that you need to be the best at everything, or that you want your name on everything, or you want the credit for everything (and, let's face it, you do). The executive team has no reason to bring someone who hogs credit or craves control or is overly competitive into their fold—why create that headache for themselves?

In addition to the perceptions perfectionists create for those above them, there is the very trying reality they create for those unlucky souls who have to work for them.

If you are constantly getting involved in work you've delegated because you need it to be right and you can't risk mistakes, you are probably coming across to others as overly critical of their work. Constructive criticism is healthy and a good path to growth, but this type of oversight isn't constructive and it creates an environment where all efforts seem futile. It's not the formula for attracting and retaining the best and the brightest!

One more point: Micro-managers are seldom as good at delegating as they think they are. It's hard to retain the control that a micromanager needs and still give the other person the authority they need to be empowered, accountable, and focused. Without some sense of autonomy and responsibility, employees don't grow. They feel stifled, start to doubt their capability, and probably see a lot of turnover around them. Even if they stick around, they are likely to have low morale.

So, yes, if you are a micromanager, peers and bosses might appreciate that you always have an answer for them right away or that you catch something that wasn't quite right that one time it really mattered, but all in all, micromanaging is not good for you and it's not good for others. Following is a quick quiz to help you recognize the impact your micromanaging tendencies might be having on those around you.

Measuring Negative Impact

Consider whether you've gotten any of the following feedback either formally or informally from your peers, staff, or bosses. If you haven't, maybe it's because you've been too mired in details to notice.

Has anyone suggested that you . . .

_____ Seem too mired in the details and have lost sight of the big picture?

_____ Are a doer (left unsaid: You aren't a leader)?

_____ Have a limited capacity for how much work you can handle? (This can limit people's confidence in your ability to take on broader roles and bigger projects.)

—— Appear to lack self-confidence because you're always working so hard?

—— Seem overly critical of others or hard on your team?

—— Can seem defensive and hurt in the face of constructive criticism?

—— Are a micro-manager?

—— Seem too risk-averse, or too reluctant to try new things or raise your visibility?

—— Don't seem responsive to others' priorities or sense of urgency on certain projects?

If you checked off any of these critiques then you have to ask yourself, what impact are you having on your organization and is it productive or useful for others? Is your perfectionism keeping you from focusing on the right things?

Solutions for the Perfectionist

If perfection, or micromanaging, is your sticky floor, you probably need to work on letting go.

Think in terms of perfecting your ability to bring out the best in your team and get the job done through them (instead of in spite of them, which might be how you often feel). Learn to let them do things on their own. And work on accepting that while others will never do things quite the same way you would, they can still do perfectly fine work. Remember the concept of "good enough" and apply it whenever you can!

Here are some more ideas for you to consider if you need help getting unstuck from this particular sticky floor:

1. Think about why you're a perfectionist. Where does the trait come from? What do you get from being a perfectionist and what does it cost you?

2. Check your standards of performance against your goals. When you create a new presentation or report, or write a memo or a team e-mail, before you do that third (or fourth or fifth) revision, ask yourself what you're trying to accomplish with it and what others have said they need from it. Then ask yourself, is this good enough to get the job done? If it is, let it go and move on (or go home!).

3. Seek feedback and use it to calibrate your own standards. That's your responsibility whenever you start something new. Talk to your internal or external customers and ask what their priorities and expectations are. What are the most critical success factors for them? What part of the project is most important to them? Use that feedback to guide the work rather than your exacting, but arbitrary standards.

4. Have a communication strategy. Once you have decided on standards and priorities for a given situation, communicate them to your team and to other key stakeholders and solicit their feedback as the project moves along. Be sure everyone understands your expectations and feels that they can be successful using them as operational guidelines.

5. Seek out peers. Identify those who are acknowledged in your organization as great leaders. Watch what they do and use that as a guide to your performance in similar situations.

6. Focus on the things that matter. Identify the things that you do that bring the most value to your organization, stakeholders, and customers. Decide what work you really need or want to do (the work that gives you visibility and showcases your leadership) and delegate the rest.

7. Let go. Develop and rely on your team. Executives develop their people so they are able to do less of the routine work and spend more of their time on planning, guiding, and attending to the strategic aspects of the business. Once you've gotten better at really delegating to your team, work on a development plan that will allow them (or select people among them) to take on more of the tasks at hand.

8. Make the hard decisions. If you are picking up slack because an employee really is a poor performer, don't ignore the fact that you made a bad hire or got stuck with dead weight. Address the performance issue by holding the employee more accountable and even letting them go if you have to. It's tough, but you're taking responsibility for making sure the people around you can deliver to the business.

Letting Go and Putting Your Abilities to Their Best Use

Pulling yourself free of the perfectionist sticky floor is a matter of shifting your point of view. You might feel that letting go of your high standards means slacking off. But it's not. It's putting as much energy and attention into work as you ever have, but putting your time to better use. You will be addressing and living up to your stakeholders' expectations rather than your own. You'll be stretching your muscles and growing instead of hurrying to stand still. And you'll be leading instead of merely doing. These are all things worthy of your energy and ability, don't you think?

Chapter 5

Making the Break

THE NEXT STICKY FLOOR, jeopardizing your personal growth and cutting off opportunities by staying in one place too long or being too loyal, is one of the easiest to fall into, and one of the most difficult to get off of because it is counterintuitive. Women who get stuck on this floor usually want to know how it can be so wrong if it feels so right.

So often, I find myself suggesting to these women that it might be time to move on to another job, in another place, with another boss and a new team. I can see the look on their faces that says deep down they know they should, but it seems so much easier to stay. And it's easy to see why. Usually, they've been in their job for several years. They are very comfortable and capable in their role, are appreciated by their boss, and feel supported by a great team. They feel important because they are the go-to person for their organization for many things. They are also the resident historian and can get things done quickly.

The problem is these women aren't advancing, and often there's no more room to grow or learn in their job. So they aren't preparing to advance either. They aren't gaining new experience, new skills, or exposure to new ideas or new people. How can you move up into the executive suite, or even closer to it, when you stay in one place? Moreover, I often meet women when they realize that they've stayed in one place too long and finally want to make a move. The trouble is, by the time they understand this, it's too late; that long stagnation is their biggest hurdle to finding something new.

Here is an example of what I mean . . .

Scenario

Sally had a great relationship with her boss, Ted, for more than five years. They worked well together and he trusted her with important tasks that he either didn't have time to do or that he thought she could do better. In his eyes, Sally was loyal, reliable, and hard working.

Their career discussions were limited. Sally just assumed that they would talk about next steps in her career when the time was right and in the meantime it was important to do a great job for her boss and the team. But Ted was on quite a different page. He assumed Sally was enjoying her job, doing work she found interesting and challenging, and that she was content to do it indefinitely.

Eventually, Ted decided it was time for him to move on and told Sally that she would be the best candidate for his replacement and that he planned to suggest her name to his boss. Sally, feeling flattered, thought that made sense and assumed she would automatically fill Ted's shoes when he left. She had preliminary discussions with Ted's manager, but several weeks later learned that the company was hiring an outsider for the job.

Sally felt betrayed. After all, she had all the functional history, knew how to get things done, knew the people, and was the elected go-to person for everything in her department. Even her former boss thought she was the best person for the job. What else were they looking for?

The problem? While Sally had Ted's praise and appreciation and her teammates loved her, she had become insular. People outside her immediate department, including Ted's boss, had a limited view of who she was and what her capabilities were. Because she assumed Ted would always look out for her, she hadn't networked and she hadn't sought opportunities that would make her visible to and valued by the other leaders in the organization—others who make the decisions about promotions.

For women who have a strong instinct to settle down and get rooted in a job, it usually comes from being socialized as a young girl to be loyal, nurturing, and supportive to others. When they find the opportunity to express these tendencies at work, it immediately appeals. They feel intrinsically rewarded and motivated to stay doing whatever it is they are doing.

In addition, it's probably what you saw your parents do. Up through the early 1980s, employees expected to stay with a single company for most of their careers. But times have changed dramatically. And while we still see some long-term employees in the middle ranks, it's not a trait you often see in executives.

The continuing trends of mergers, acquisitions, and reorganizations with their accompanying reshuffling of executive teams has put a new light on the realities of career advancement. In addition, in a global marketplace where all kinds of diversity are seen as bringing potential value, the more different companies and people you've been exposed to, and the more you've worked in different parts of the country or even different parts of the world, the more likely you are to be understanding, making use of and appealing to different points of view.

The Myths About Staying in One Place Too Long

Table 5-1 shows some outdated career myths and some of the new realities that are important to understand:

Table 5-1

Career Myth	Career Reality
Most people follow traditional career paths through their organization.	Career paths are not straight and narrow today. We need to assert more focus and accountability to managing our own advancement.
Top performers who work the hardest advance most rapidly in the organization.	Hard work and good performance are not the only criteria for getting to the top. Having a broader understanding of the business and building a broad network of relationships is just as important. Other people's perceptions of your value, capabilities, and desire to advance are also critical.
Staying with one mentor or sponsor/advocate within a company can greatly improve your ability to advance there.	Relying on one mentor or sponsor can limit your perspective on the company's business and can keep you from hearing about potential opportunities elsewhere in the organization. It also limits your opportunities to get the word out about you. Today you need to have multiple mentors in addition to your boss.
Earning bonuses and performance awards is a ticket to the executive suite and is a good indicator of your chances for promotion.	What you are being recognized for today may not be what they are looking for on the executive team tomorrow. Skill sets might be different and impressions of you in terms of the critical success factors for senior management need to be managed carefully.
People who have spent more than 10 years with the same organization have a strong track record for reliability and credibility, which makes them a sure bet for the executive suite.	Many of today's successful executives have a diverse mix of work experiences. They have proven themselves in several organizations, which can make them seem more broadly competent. When it comes to competing for the top jobs, they have an advantage over internal candidates with narrower experience.

A Look at Your Track Record

Now don't get me wrong. There are many good reasons to stay in one place for a little while. There's the opportunity to nurture others and watch them grow, the chance to learn and become an expert in a particular part of a business, the opportunity to have close relation-ships with a team and boss, and to demonstrate that you aren't fickle—not to mention the financial reward of staying someplace long enough to get options, stock grants, or retirement funds.

Why and when should you leave all that? It depends on you and your situation. Below are exercises and anecdotes to help become a better judge of when you are in danger of getting too rooted down and what you can do about it.

A Quick Test

To assess whether you might be overdue for a new opportunity, take the following test. Check off any of the situations that ring true about you.

_____ You feel unsure of the future of your organization.

_____ You feel that your progress within the company is limited or is somehow being blocked by conditions outside of your control.

_____ You feel that you are not being challenged or learning anymore.

_____ You feel you are not being appropriately recognized for your value and contributions in ways that matter (like promotions or high-profile stretch assignments).

_____ You feel pigeon-holed. Everyone knows you as the expert in a certain area, but you get passed over for opportuni-ties that would use other knowledge or experience you have.

If you checked any of these questions, it might be time to move on. You're quickly outgrowing your job (if you haven't already) and if you want to continue to develop and expand your professional skills, then you need a new environment where you can cultivate different skills, experience new opportunities, and work with a new group of people.

At the very least, you need to think about asserting your individual brand and being recognized for your individual potential instead of allowing yourself to be identified solely with one group or person (your boss).

If I Do a Good Job, I Will Be Promoted When the Time Is Right

For many women, the hardest part about getting off this sticky floor—or maybe even recognizing they are on a sticky floor—is breaking down the belief that their effort and good work are always apparent to everyone and will be rewarded in due course. This just isn't true. We sometimes feel that people should know what we want or, in some cases, should read our minds. We speak in code—maybe talk about how hard we worked and what we got done—but does that really let people know our true aspirations or career goals or even frustrations?

Even if your boss and immediate co-workers appreciate your capabilities and productivity, that doesn't mean people beyond your most immediate circle have any insight into your capabilities. Nor will those other people necessarily make an effort to learn about you—why should they when they have so much else going on around them? There are several ways that being loyal to one person or group and patiently waiting for your time to come can backfire.

Let me give you a few examples.

First, you might be doing a great job and hitting all of your objectives, and your boss and team might appreciate your abilities and give you good feedback. That doesn't mean they are necessarily discussing your good work with others in the organization who might have opportunities or control promotions you are interested in. But it's not their job to talk you up; it's your job. Even if you are happy where you are for the time being, it's important to lay the groundwork for future moves by networking and making your work, skills and interests known to others.

Secondly, if you are doing a great job and aren't expressing any interest in advancing in your career, your boss can naturally assume that you are happy with what you are doing and aren't looking to do something else. Even if you aren't looking to move ahead at full speed at the moment, you need to raise the question of your long-term development with your boss to set an expectation for what you want to see happen with your career over the long term. That's the only failsafe way to make your boss responsible for your professional development.

Third, there are times when a person is too good to lose. If your boss depends on you a great deal, he or she might not want to lose you! I think many managers want to hold on to a good thing and therefore don't look for opportunities to promote their star performers unless someone (you) brings it to their attention that they need to be doing this.

Finally, you can also lose your marketability if you stay in one place too long. People put a box around what you are good at and stop expecting you to move beyond that. People who don't know you might also wonder why you stayed in one place too long and suspect that you might have tried to move and some lack of ability or know-how has held you back, even if that isn't true.

The bottom line is that having broader business expertise, more diverse work experience and greater exposure is always going to serve you better in the long run than going out of your way to limit your experience and exposure.

Getting Out of Your Comfort Zone—Face Your Fears and Walk Through Them

There are people who love change and thrive on it. But they aren't most people. The majority of us prefer to not have to deal with change and put it off as long as we can. After all, it carries uncertainty and uncertainty usually carries risk. Risk aversion is a very natural instinct. So it's no surprise that men and women can become very skilled at justifying why they remain in a particular job.

But women have a particular vulnerability that drives our loyalty too far and that's the caregiver factor. As wives heading households, mothers raising children, or daughters caring for aging parents, women often feel guilty about asking what they believe is too much from their bosses—flexible hours, family leave, the ability to telecommute. Some even feel guilty for actually using *all* their vacation time each year. These women can feel that, because a boss has been "so great," they owe it to their employer to stick around and be loyal. Or they fear that at a new company, where they haven't yet proven themselves, they will have less latitude to preserve the fragile work-life balance they've built.

The problem is that if you stay in one job, sooner or later, personal growth stalls and frustration, stress, self-doubt, and loss of self-esteem creep in. This is the worst-case scenario: Women come to realize they need a change, but in a way that leaves them feeling vulnerable. As a result, achieving change seems like a Herculean and incredibly fraught task.

I think it might be valuable to remind these change-averse caregivers that the bottom line always drives decisions. Employers hold on to and hire the people who can bring the greatest value and perspective to their mission. If they let you have an extra long leave, a compressed workweek, or a flexible schedule, it wasn't *just* to be nice and do you a favor. On some level, the company or manager who gave you that latitude believed your skills or performance made the compromise worthwhile. If they didn't believe you could still do your job and add value or that it wouldn't work for them, they most likely would not have done it. As long as you've pulled your weight and done a good job all along, you owe them as much loyalty as any other employee, but not necessarily any more. And it's as reasonable for you as for any other employee to consider opportunities to advance yourself.

And as for potential new employers, well it's not really fair to assume they won't be able to work with your flexible schedule before you even talk to them. Flex work is so common today that many companies use it as a recruiting tool. So you've got nothing to lose by getting out in front of people, telling them what you have to offer, and letting them know your bottom line, be it a four-day week or working from home in the morning. Give them the opportunity to say *yes* rather than assuming they will say *no*.

If change itself seems too overwhelming to think about, take inspiration from Wendy Hufford, who left her job as senior global litigation counsel of General Electric, in Westchester, New York, to become chief litigation counsel of Cardinal Health, in Dublin, Ohio. In addition to being an accomplished attorney, Wendy is also the mother of eight and the wife of an equally successful attorney. Changing jobs didn't just mean leaving a great company, but relocating the entire family, her husband's job, and several pets. She told *Corporate Counsel* that the thought of quitting her previous job was as daunting as the prospect of moving, but Cardinal was offering her a "dream job." Everything from winning the kids over to the idea of moving to settling in to the new job went much more smoothly than she had expected. She told the magazine that the lesson she took from the experience was, "Don't be afraid to take a chance to pursue your career dreams—and enjoy the ride."

The Leap of Faith

No matter what your situation, once you decide to make a career move, the hard work really begins, and it can be very emotional. Particularly in these uncertain times, leaving a steady job, regular paycheck, and good work-life situation for an unknown and unproven opportunity can seem like courting danger—better the devil you know than the devil you don't, right?

But those people who take the risks and gain diverse experiences end up knowing more. They have more opportunities open to them, are more employable, and make better money. I learned from experience that taking a leap of faith and making a change can be the best opportunity for growth and development. Once you do it the first time, the rest is easy.

Consider the thought process I went through after leaving a good job with Amax, Inc., where I had been director of human resources for five years. I knew after only three years in that job that I needed to expand my skills beyond recruiting and other limited human resource functions the job covered. But I loved the work, had a good boss and great people working with me, and lived near family and good friends.

Fortunately—in a way—the decision to move on was made for me; I was laid off. The unemployment rate in Indiana was 15 percent, so I knew the chances of advancing to a greater level of responsibility while staying in Indiana were not great. I did receive an offer to work in Chicago, a bigger city and one I'd always loved. It was a small step up and a little more money, but it was also very similar to the job I'd left and wouldn't advance my career all that much.

While I was weighing the Chicago offer, I got a call one night from a man who headed up human resources for Fairchild Industries outside of Washington, D.C. He was looking for a replacement for his job and had heard about me from a mutual colleague. This position was a huge jump in scope and experience level from what I had been doing. Moreover, it would require me to move from the Midwest, where I had lived all my life, to the East Coast, where I knew no one.

Moving away from my family, friends, and a boyfriend would require a big leap of faith, and the odds were not all in my favor. But it was the opportunity of a lifetime; one that would offer challenges, and opportunities to grow, learn, and experience an area of the country that seemed exciting and different from where I had lived.

I did a self-analysis, asking myself how this job would align with my career goals. I considered the worst that could happen if I didn't succeed in the new job, or didn't get along with my new boss, or didn't like the Washington, D.C., area. I considered how I would handle being separated from family and friends.

After anguishing for several days over whether to take the familiar and definitely manageable step or the dizzying leap, I knew that my thought process was more emotional than rational. What it mostly came down to was fear about leaving so many things I'd been comfortable with for so many years. I realized that while they were near and dear to me, holding on to the familiar too strongly could limit my opportunities to grow and prosper. I dug deeper and did a more rational risk factor analysis and began to see all those changes as opportunities, rather than dangers. Opening to change would allow me to advance and have more opportunities in both the short and long run.

So I decided to give Washington a chance. I would go for two years and then decide whether to stay or reconnect with colleagues in Indiana. I ended up staying there for more than six years and loved the job. It definitely provided an accelerated learning curve and made me more marketable, mature, and confident. It also opened the door to numerous great relationships that I still have. To this day, I can recall how scary the decision was, but I'm grateful that I found it within me to take that leap.

My experience is a great example of how easy it is to stay in your comfort zone and how important it is to push yourself beyond it, at least periodically.

Balancing What Exists with the Future

We sometimes get caught up in the moment and in the short run make good choices but sometimes don't consider the long-term perspective. Maybe you can't have that dream of wanting to be partner or EVP right now because of your need to spend more time with your children or elderly parents. But what do children or taking care of your elderly parents have to do with five years from now? You don't have to give up your whole career dream. We sometimes become too pragmatic about what exists right now versus the possibility of the future. It is hard when you feel torn, in conflict, or just over the top with juggling so many balls. And it is good to set priorities and act on them as they present themselves in life. But I suggest to you that it does not have to be all or nothing. It could be that you decide to shift to part time for a while and be the "best" three-day person your organization has ever had.

At the very least, keep in mind that nothing stays the same. You might not be able to see a time when you aren't thrilled to be right where you are now. But remember, your kids could go off to college and with fewer personal demands on your personal life, you might find you want more from your job again. Like Sally, your boss might leave and that could change your work situation entirely. Your company could be acquired or go through a reorganization that changes, shrinks, or eliminates your job. It's always better to leap and choose change than to be pushed and have change thrust upon you.

I learned from my Fairchild experience that complacency is often a good way to cover up a fear of change. But once you take that first leap of faith, you begin to develop a muscle that makes you less intimidated by the unfamiliar. You don't become less afraid. But still, each time a risky opportunity comes along it's a little easier to put aside your irrational fears and go ahead with it.

The Leadership Factor

Actively seeking out new opportunities and learning to tolerate risk is a form of leadership, in that being a good leader is about putting yourself in different and challenging experiences that teach you new things about yourself and the world in which you work. An early mentor shared that I would never be a complete leader who knows all I need to know. Developing leadership is a continuous journey and you should always be learning, changing, and growing. That view has helped me to supplant my fear with curiosity. This gives me inner confidence in situations where I might not otherwise have it, and that in turn allows other people to trust and have confidence in me, too.

Steps for Dealing with Fear

You've read about some of the things that encourage women to stay in one place too long and keep them from proactively moving on. If you believe you have been limiting yourself unnecessarily, it might be valuable to walk through a process that helps women to get unstuck.

Consider the following scenario.

Suppose someone tells you about a job opening that sparks your interest and he or she even suggests that you interview for it. It is a more senior position than the job you have now and would require new skills. It's also at a company for which you've never worked. There are new players and you have no way of knowing if you'll work well with them. You might be concerned that you won't learn the new skills quickly enough, that you won't like the new company, won't get along with the new boss, or you'll lose your friends from your current job. What will you do?

I think for many of us, we hold back and avoid taking that leap into a new or more challenging role because we have such high standards. We may have an opportunity to consider a broader level of responsibility but we sometimes end up saying that we are not confident in that job—too much of a stretch based on what we know now, so we end up staying where we are. Sometimes our instinct will probably be to pull back and stay where we feel safe, know the job, and have little room to fail or let others down. This is a common reaction for many women. Why? First, women have a tendency to *overanalyze* the risk. While it is good to be prudent, this can also be a limiting factor for advancement. Successful women say that their biggest regret was not taking that risk or leap sooner. Much of what held them back was that inner voice saying, "I am not totally familiar with some of the new skills needed for the job," or, "What if I let someone down?" Or, "Not now, I need to go back to school and in a few years I'll be ready." They needed to be totally ready and fully competent.

If you have executive suite aspirations, you have to learn to suppress that instinct, leave emotions out of the equation, and focus on objectively sizing up what the opportunity can or can't do for your career.

Here are five questions that will help you to take an objective view:

1. What can happen short and long term if I take the new job?

2. What do I lose short term and long term if I don't take it?

3. What can I gain if I take it and it works?

4. What do I lose if I take it and it does not work?

5. What are some contingency plans if it does not work?

Making a change or taking a risk is most risky if you haven't thought through what you are getting into. But, once you break down both the positives and negatives and you begin to think through all the things you can do to prevent things from going wrong or to recover if they do, you begin to feel much more in control of the situation and you begin to feel more confident about being able to manage the unknowns. My advice is, consider the worst case, maybe the job doesn't work out, but maybe you get closer to where you want to be.

Talking to someone—anyone—about your concerns and the opportunity will also help you to put things in perspective. Listening to yourself talk about the job to that other person will probably tell you how you really feel about it. Are you excited more than anything else when it comes down to it, or is there a lingering concern that tells you that *this* opportunity isn't the right one? At the very least, you'll probably learn that everyone feels afraid when they face change, and knowing that fear is normal will also make it less intimidating and more within your control.

Don't Wait for It to Happen: Have a Plan, or Someone Will Have One for You

In addition to covering up for fear, complacency is also a good cover for procrastination and inaction. It's easier to be happy where you are than to even *think* about developing a plan for where you could be. With all the things most people have to do in a day, who even has time to sketch out a life plan and start strategizing about it? Some call this ambition, but really it gets down to knowing what you want and just going for it. Waiting for some vague future opportunity to come to you works much better with most people's schedules. The most successful men and women executives were strategic in terms of their careers. They were proactive—meaning they had a goal to get from point A to point B to point C. For some of us, this is difficult because it is not our nature to be aggressive or competitive, but rather more collaborative. For example, we sometimes prefer to have someone else come to us and share their view of our talents and potential. We then consider those greater opportunities, versus investing time to become more aware of our own hidden strengths and desires and taking accountability for what we really want. It sometimes seems more natural for our boss to come to us and say, "I really see you as a strong managing director."

But consider this question that I routinely ask the women I coach: Who would you rather have influence your next job or shape your career path for the next decade, you or someone else?

Whoever that someone else might be, that person probably won't have the same grasp on your desires, motivations, and strengths that you do. This person might frame the so-called opportunities presented to you around the open boxes that need to be filled, rather than around your needs and desires. Or worse, this person might just see your work as a vehicle for furthering his or her career without any consideration for yours.

Of course, the answer to the question is that you are better off in your own driver's seat. Once again, this takes us back to the need to pause—just briefly—from the day-to-day details to think about a long-term and short-term plan.

Yes, the vision thing—men and women who are executive suite material think out the next job long before they even raise their hand for it.

I had one woman I was coaching who always talked about what she wanted her last job to be. She wanted to oversee the human resources for a major organization and she wanted a seven-figure salary. We talked on a regular basis about the interim jobs that would get her there, and whenever a new opportunity came up I would ask her, "Is this job the next stepping-stone toward your ultimate goal?"

Following is a shorthand version of the analysis I went through with her, to get you thinking about your career more strategically and proactively.

1. Take a step back and define your ultimate career goals and objectives. Think big and don't let obstacles stand in your way. For example, if you are vice president or senior director of Finance, is your final destination a chief financial officer position?

2. Now, write down the experiences and knowledge you have acquired so far in your current and past jobs.

3. Next, identify the skills and knowledge areas you want to continue to learn about and any new skills or experiences you want to begin to cultivate.

4. Ask yourself which of these are things you won't be able to build or acquire in the job you have now?

5. Pull it all together. Is there still some room for you to develop yourself, take new risks and have new experiences in your current job? Or have you made the most of it and "plateaued" by now? If you know there isn't much more you can get from your current position, then it's time to look around. Is it possible to find new growth opportunities at your current organization and is the internal move you would want to make doable? Or would it be better to move on completely and experience a new organization?

Even if you don't see any opportunities within your organization to further advance yourself toward your end game, you don't necessarily have to start calling recruiters and begin job hunting. Instead, schedule conversations with your boss and with other influential people in your organization with whom you have good, trusting relationships. Your introduction should go something like this:

I have enjoyed my job here at the company and feel like I am making a good contribution for you and the organization. But I wanted to let you know that I am not entirely satisfied with what I am doing and where it is taking me. My goal is to be a chief financial officer. Here are some areas I would like to work in that would help me to further develop and prepare for that role. I would welcome your ideas and perceptions, and I hope we can come up with a plan for my career here. If that's not possible, I may need to consider options outside of the organization.

The discussion you are setting up with this summation should bring more objectivity and focus to your strategizing and planning. And it should help you to have a constructive conversation with people who can help you to shape and develop your career. It helps you to pursue a conversation that will be less emotional and more businesslike. The response you receive might not be what you are hoping for or what you expect, and you need to be prepared for that. But, for better or for worse, it will clarify the should-I-stay-or-should-I-go discussion going on in your head and take the anguish out of your decision.

The Next Job . . . and the Next One

If you've decided it's time to move to a new job in your company or to a new company, then you need a good framework for sizing up the opportunities you seek and create for yourself. To that end, you ought to think about what you want your next *two* jobs to be. Figure out how to get the first one, then the second one.

Here's a realistic timeframe: In year one, you are learning the job. In year two, you are doing it well and producing results and making meaningful connections with people in your new circle. In year three, you'll want to start looking at what else you can do in that job to build toward your overall plan. It's also time to start discussing opportunities for job number two with your new boss and other people inside or outside your organization who might be able to create that opportunity for you.

Following are a few questions to think about when considering your next moves:

1. What is the dream job or end goal you set out for yourself earlier in the chapter?

2. What skills or experiences do you still need to add to your resume to prepare you for that role?

3. What kinds of jobs will give you that experience? Could a single new position do it or will you need a few different jobs, perhaps with different types of organizations or in different locations to accumulate the right experience and skills?

4. Are you looking for sequential positions with increasingly broader or bigger responsibilities? Or will you need a series of lateral moves that cumulatively will provide the right mix of experiences?

5. Of those several next jobs you'd like, which one makes the most sense to go after first? And second?

6. What experiences or skills do you need to make sure you develop in the first job to best position yourself for the second one?

7. What will you need from both of them to make sure that together they move you toward your end goal?

8. How does this line of thinking frame your next job hunt? What sorts of jobs will you say *yes* to, and which ones will you turn down?

Yes, They Can Get Along Without You

Sharon Allen, chairman of Deloitte & Touche USA, says that many women stay put for too long because they feel guilty about leaving. They feel they are abandoning those they have worked with for so long.

Sharon points out that this might come from the knowledge that they've routinely helped their boss look good, or they've mentored or coached someone on their team and feel responsible for their continued success. Sometimes they've progressed quickly enough to pass others by and are concerned about hard feelings.

"The reality," Sharon says, "is that once you move on, people will thrive and grow more than you could have possibly imagined. By leaving, you are creating a need that will have to be filled, but that generates opportunities for others to step up and grow." Sharon recalls a boss who mentored her well and eventually stepped out of his job as managing partner, allowing her to fill his shoes. "He let me in and he moved on," she says. If he'd felt guilty about abandoning her, he would have in effect put a cap on her opportunities at the firm.

It's true that no one is indispensable. So take care of your career, make the moves that you know you need to make to get yourself to the executive suite, and trust that everything will take care of itself.

It's also true that for anyone to grow and advance in a career, they have to be willing to be uncomfortable from time to time. It's pivotal for women to understand that breaking their own glass ceiling will sometimes require them to take calculated risks and step out of their comfort zone. Finding yourself in this situation is not a sign of incompetence—quite the contrary. It's a sign that you're going in the right direction.

I encourage you to look for opportunities to leverage what you can do into something bigger, or at least broader. Trust that the right people will look up to you if you take control of your career and make the moves that you know you need to get yourself closer to the executive suite. And trust that everyone else will take care of themselves.

Chapter 6

Forming Your Own Board of Directors

You can do so little alone and so much together. —HELEN KELLER

Strategic Relationships Matter

There is no question in my mind that women naturally have a lot of friends and relationships in their life, but when I ask women if they have the right people for advising and helping them to progress in their career or to help them achieve the goals they need to within their organization, most of them say no. When I ask whether they have *strategic relationships* they sometimes get frustrated or even turned off. Why? Oftentimes they feel that having strategic relationships seems manipulative and self-serving, or they truly think they can do it on their own, and that it's easier that way.

But when I speak to audiences on this topic, I ask them to think of a major accomplishment in their life, one they feel exceptionally good about. Then I ask them if they were really able to accomplish it on their own. Nine times out of ten, people say no, they had one or several people who were instrumental in helping them get there.

This chapter is about building *relationships*. I don't mean manipulative, impersonal, or self-serving relationships, but mutually beneficial ones that provide both people with opportunities to learn, grow, advance in their careers, and bring greater value to others around them. Such good, strategic relationships allow leaders to better contribute on important initiatives for their team, organization, and the world. That might sound hyperbolic, but I really do believe that once you enter the executive suite you have the opportunity to do big things, and it is all about relationships.

A lot of women have advanced in their careers by capitalizing on a strong command of a particular technical skill and keeping their nose to the grindstone to get results from their team and meet their functional objectives. All well and good, however, I find that one of the biggest hurdles to overcome in moving beyond functional roles, to senior levels of leadership, is learning to deal with an organization's more strategic issues. Many leaders and executives find that when transitioning to these broader roles they need fewer analytical, task-oriented skills and more relationship-building skills.

Regina Sommors, a colleague of mine and woman executive, points out that among people competing for the most senior jobs, knowledge is something of a commodity. Everyone has an impeccable and impressive set of skills and credentials, so having the right relationships becomes even more important for meeting your goals and getting your name out there to the right people. Additionally, the CEO of a major healthcare organization once told me that when he looks for good people for his team, he assumes competence in everyone he talks to. Instead of focusing on skills or experience, he looks for people he knows, trusts, likes, and believes will have good chemistry with the rest of his team.

There are several distinct and interdependent relationships that bring unique support and value at different times based on one's goals, challenges, and opportunities that leaders deal with on a daily basis. This point was indicated in a *Harvard Business Review* article, "How Leaders Create and Use Networks," by Herminia Ibarra and Mark Hunter. The article said that when it comes to managing transition, there are several distinct, but interdependent, forms of relationships or networks—operational, personal, and strategic. These networks played a vital role for the managers and leaders the authors interviewed. The operational network helped managers to build good working relationships with the people who can help them do their jobs—to manage their current internal responsibilities. The personal network helped them to boost their personal development outside of their usual circles through professional associations, alumni groups, and personal interest committees. These relationships helped them to gain a new perspective that allowed them to advance in their broader profession. The strategic network helped managers to open their eyes to new business directions and the stakeholders they would need to enlist. These would include lateral and vertical relationships with other functional and business unit managers that helped the manager to achieve important personal and organizational goals.

Having an integrated and diverse network of people is a smart and practical way to balance and develop relationships at any career stage. For example, you might have great and supportive relationships inside the organization, but might also be too insular in your focus. An accomplished woman executive asked me to lunch and said she was leaving her organization after 23 great years and was looking to pursue something different. She said that while she had great and supportive relationships inside the company, she realized that she had failed to foster external relationships with peers, industry groups, and professional organizations. She felt as though she was starting from scratch. She felt out of touch and didn't know where to start in terms of building that important network for taking on another job outside of her company. In Ibarra and Hunter's article they said, "Savvy people reach out to kindred spirits outside of their organization to contribute and multiply their knowledge, and the information they glean, in more cases than not, becomes the 'hook' for making internal connections. Conversely, a person can be too focused on external relationships and overlook essential internal relationships that could have a positive impact on her key initiatives for the company or keep her tuned into the strategic approach and direction of the company." Ensuring you have the right balance of relationships is important so you have the right blend of people to provide the right support and perspective as opportunities and situations present themselves.

When I look at corporate leaders I admire, who have good credibility, leadership ability, and power, I see how they have surrounded themselves with a diverse and rich pool of people on whom they can rely. On the way up the ladder, they put time into knowing the smart and talented people and then worked on creating the right mix of backgrounds, perspectives, and levels of influence they need in order to achieve great things.

Carly Fiorina says in her book, *Tough Choices* (Penguin Group, 2006), that people don't do business with companies, they do business with other people. In other words, at all levels, business is driven by people. How well executives manage their relationships directly determines how successful a company will be and how effective they will be as leaders.

I can also speak to this from personal experience. As I've made my way through my corporate human resources career and later, through growing a business, I've cultivated a diverse and rich blend of people who have stretched my thinking and challenged my assumptions. Among them, different people have been crucial advisers and advocates at different stages.

For example, about seven years ago I noticed that my network hadn't changed or grown much in a while and that I was due to put some energy into cultivating a broader spectrum of relationships. Around that time, I was invited to one of the bigger and more popular golf events in the greater Washington, D.C., area. It seemed like the kind of opportunity I was looking for to make some new contacts, but I had no clue how to play (and I always suspected it was a boring and time-consuming pastime).

Nevertheless, in the spirit of career advancement and open-mindedness, I reached out to a fellow CEO colleague who was good at golf. I explained to him that I wanted to learn how to play well enough to not embarrass myself or the rest of my foursome if I went out to play a round with business acquaintances. And I asked if he knew of any golf pros for lessons.

He suggested I go out to play a round first to make sure I enjoyed it, at least a little, and offered to take me out on the course the next weekend. I managed to get the ball off the tee and onto the fairway and actually enjoyed the afternoon. I could see why it's a good sport for business—there's a lot of downtime while you're moving from hole to hole or waiting for others to tee off where you can talk and get to know another person. So my friend connected me to his pro and I signed up in time to have a few lessons before the tournament.

In the meantime, my friend introduced me to several members of the club, which made my investment in golf and in my relationship with him pay off almost immediately. I'm still playing (and even have a reasonable handicap) and have joined a club where I invite business associates to dine with me or play golf. This wouldn't have happened if I hadn't made that first phone call.

But it hasn't been a one-way street. These relationships have also provided me with an opportunity to give to others. For example, I've referred several of my friends and colleagues to that golf pro. While this might not have helped my CEO friend directly, it did help someone in his network (who was also now in my network) and signaled to him that I appreciated the connection.

Strategic versus Personal Relationships

What's the difference between strategic and personal relationships?

Personal relationships are anchored in the emotional ties you have to family and friends. They're grounded in the personal experiences and interests you share with those people and are less about your work. When I think about strategic relationships, I focus on building relationships with a specific purpose or goal in mind. Strategic relationships can run as long and deep as your personal ones but are usually more narrowly focused.

Being *strategic* means making active decisions about which possible new relationships you would like to cultivate at any given time based on the career or business goals you are trying to achieve. Some will last for years while others might come and go.

For example, say you're an executive moving to a new house and you know you want to make it the best space possible for a home office as well as for entertaining clients and colleagues. Should you happen to meet an interior designer at a cocktail party, you would probably take her card—not because you think you'll develop a 20-year relationship with her, but because she might be able to offer valuable advice or referrals or services to you over the next few months.

On the other hand, an entrepreneur might have ongoing relationships with the CFO of her former employer who advises her on the financial issues she occasionally faces, a former classmate who is in human resources and advises her on hiring and training issues, and a circle of local entrepreneurs in complimentary businesses who commiserate with one another and refer clients back and forth.

In the corporate world, good relationships will allow you to learn more about what's going on in other parts of your company or industry. They can help you to influence others, align your goals with those of the organization's, and feed the internal radar you need to not be caught off guard by significant changes or developments that might be afoot.

Here's what I mean:

Sally's organization was about to be involved in a merger, but she hadn't heard anything about it. She was known as being an A player within her division, but she had not taken the time to build relationships outside of her small domain, so the executive group and leaders in other parts of the organization weren't at all familiar with her abilities. When the merger came she ended up with a minor role in the new company that carried less visibility, responsibility, and influence than she'd had before.

Worse, the company filled Sally's old job with a guy named John, who had been involved with the merger discussions early on and who had talked to a lot of people about the forthcoming changes, what talent the top executives were going to need, and who the key decision-makers would be in the reorganization. John also scheduled time with the top leadership to do a formal proposal about where he thought he could bring value and align with the new company.

A key lesson from Sally is that it is important to reach out to others to make sure they have information and they need about you. John networked to get information and guidance he could use, but along the way he also provided information that they needed and that he wanted them to have.

Have Your Own Board of Directors

You've heard of the idea that everyone needs their own board of directors, or board of advisers, or kitchen cabinet, but such a group really is essential. It helps you avoid a lot of headaches and mistakes, and it helps you to get more out of your life and work. The members of my board include my father, who is a fellow entrepreneur, colleagues in my profession, and the trusted, long-time employees I rely on to keep SHAMBAUGH running from day to day.

As I've grown my company, my board has complemented my weaknesses by lending me knowledge or skills that I need from time to time. They've also connected me to a greater sphere of people than I would not have had access to otherwise. In addition to my long-time constants, there have been people who have come to the forefront during one crucial stage but who later faded away. For example, there was a recruiter who helped me see that, more than a new job, I really wanted to strike out on my own and he actually coached me through the transition from corporate manager to entrepreneur.

Such *good strategic relationships* are not developed overnight, though, and they don't appear at one's front door when you need them. They take time, commitment, and energy to grow into something beneficial.

Chris Hipwell, who works in executive sales for Pfizer, says, "We sometimes work in isolation because we want all the glory and recognition. That is impossible. We are now evaluated on how we build an inclusive and collaborative environment." She continues, "You can't do it alone. When we put so much time into something all on our own and it doesn't work, we wonder why it didn't. It's because we didn't get others on board—get their endorsement. People can be strategic about the business, but not strategic about relationships. Why? It takes time to step back and look at the puzzle board and figure out the relationships we need to not only identify with but reach out to."

Chris says that building strategic relationships calls for mapping out a web of people who can help you with something you need or are trying to do. "You have to be realistic. Know that it can take time to connect with and influence people in your web. Sometimes people will give up and say it takes too long or that they don't know where to start."

For her part, Chris says that she often will tap on her sphere of relationships when she needs money to fund something in her organization:

The first thing I need to think about is, who also needs this and who would benefit from this if it was a success. Then you need to know who would have a bias—potential resisters. At Pfizer you are expected to figure out who you need to get on board for whatever you are trying to drive or propose. If you have a senior vice president who is totally behind your program and an executive vice president of sales is not, it's important to build a bridge with both, but particularly the one who is going to carry the biggest influence and who may not be behind you. So in this case you need to build a bridge and reach out to the executive vice president of sales.

Where Women Fall Short

While women have a knack for developing trusting and supportive relationships, they sometimes lack the broader network within or outside of their organization that can help them achieve their goals and objectives.

Often, women have a tendency to keep their head down and make sure they are doing a great job, even as they are rising through the ranks. They underestimate how important the right relationships can be in getting ahead, getting initiatives done, and accomplishing objectives. And they play down the concerted effort a person has to make to seek out and cultivate these relationships.

Anne Reed, president of Acquisition Solutions and former president of state and local business at EDS, said this:

> As a business executive you need to deal with a lot of issues and objectives that require a broad spectrum of knowledge and expertise on a regular basis. Therefore, you need to know a lot of people versus just a few people. There is rarely a day or week where I don't need to pick up the phone and ask a question or need help with something. In some cases, women feel that a relationship is a relationship only if it has depth to it with a rich tenor, whereas men will look at relationships as not having to be that deep. While

deep and close relationships are important, we sometimes limit ourselves in getting the support we need by keeping relationships close and sometimes too personal.

You know the guys in your organization who seem to always go out for lunch no matter what's going on—and you wonder how they can blow off their jobs to schmooze? They see lunch as part of their job. They're making a conscious effort to spend part of their day connecting with others and if you look closely you'll see that, one way or another, the work gets done. They're getting the work done *and* building the relationships. This might be why they seem to have an easier time getting the good assignments, promotions, or job offers. That's why you see them leaving work early to go to a baseball game or to play a round of golf. Getting out of the office and spending time with customers, partners, and other important colleagues can sometimes be a more effective and productive way to learn about someone. Anne Reed says she started to spend time—during the business day—playing golf with people because she found that you can learn a lot about people and they can learn a lot about you this way. After a round of golf, you can learn whether they are team players or too competitive, what's important to them, and their strongest characteristics. It may help you to decide if you want to do business with them. Anne said jokingly, "When I see someone who keeps picking up his or her ball and moving it to a better position, beware—that is a warning about their internal motivations."

What I have found is that men who are in executive-level jobs, tend to reinvent themselves and land a new job sometimes sooner than women. Much of this is due to the fact that men already have an outside and supportive network that they can tap into. In general, women have lacked the broader and more strategic networks which can make it difficult or prolongs the time it takes to make a successful career transition.

It's understandable why some women might have difficulty building relationships for specific purposes. As young girls, we were socialized to include everybody in our play activities, and the worst things you could be labeled on the playground were a "user" or a "phony."

Boys seemed less likely to vilify one another for being pragmatic about their relationships. So men are more likely to view relationships as transactional—they're okay connecting with someone for the simple purpose of getting something done, or having someone connect with them that way.

Women feel a need to connect and are less comfortable reaching out and building a network of relationships with people with whom they might have nothing in common. Some will tell me it seems too superficial. Others are too accustomed to being the capable nurturer to feel comfortable asking for help. Others worry about whether they deserve the boost or favor they're asking for and believe they'll be asked to justify or prove themselves to have it granted.

So, how do you get over these fears of rejection, of being unfairly labeled, or doing something unacceptable? When we talk about building strategic relationships in our WILL program, we ask the women participants to ask themselves how they view and use their relationships. After they begin to answer the following questions, they realize they are not as focused on building and fostering the right relationships for their own benefit and success. Here are a few questions that you can answer to better understand how well you are using your relationships around you.

1. Do you normally try to do and conquer things on your own, or do you reach out to others, even though it means you might not be able to own all the success and glory?

2. In your work, do you have a broad network of acquaintances or a few very close relationships?

3. Do you consciously make time to build the right relationships on a daily basis?

4. Do you hold back in reaching out for support because you feel people won't have time for you? Do you reach out and propose a time to talk or meet on the other person's terms and schedule?

5. Do you consider or use strategic relationships for self-development?

6. If you can, identify a time when you had a relationship that helped you to achieve something important. Was that easier than it would have been doing it on your own?

7. How often do you collaborate with others to support what they want or need? How do you feel when you're asked?

8. When you ask for support do people respond positively, or do they seem confused and shrug you off?

9. How well do you prepare and think through what you want and how to ask for that support?

10. Have you relied on the same network of supportive relationships for some time?

11. Do you typically wait until you have a need for support and then ask someone, or do you build relationships ahead of time?

Your answers to these questions should begin to generate ideas and conclusions about your past experiences and encourage you to cultivate and capitalize on your professional relationships more.

I want to point out in this part of the chapter that we all have an enormous capacity for building deep-rooted relationships that can have a wonderful and positive impact on everyone involved. How well we capitalize on this ability is based on our own assumptions and beliefs about relationships. All of the successful women executives I have interviewed and met along the way view having strategic relationships from the spirit of collaboration and mutual support. These are substantive relationships that take time and energy to build, but it can be done in an authentic way that results in meaningful and productive outcomes for the greater good. And yes, they should also have a positive impact on your career and well-being. If you haven't already learned that having the right relationships at the right time is an essential factor for self-development and career advancement, this chapter should demonstrate that to you.

The Law of Reciprocity

For some women it becomes easier to reach out to others and ask for help or advice or information when they realize that it isn't a one-way street; that they really do have something to offer the other person, or at the very least are in a position to "return the favor" down the road. They understand that not only is there a "law of reciprocity," but that they can exercise it.

But I'll go one step further to say that I have found that the more I help others, the more help I receive in return. I don't keep tally of what I do or look for quid pro quo, but if I help someone and bring him or her something of value, it's almost certain that they'll remember it and want to return that value to me.

For example, I mentored a young woman for close to two years. We met for lunches and I invited her to certain functions or events that I thought she would find valuable. She later let me know that she had moved to a new company in a job that she was very excited about. Two years later, I got a call from her and she invited me to lunch to meet one of the executives of her organization. I had no real expectations but, through her introduction, my firm wound up working with her organization on several programs for their women leaders. This is just one example of how my reaching out and providing value or support for others opened up unexpected doors for me.

It's great to be able to give before you need to receive, but if you do need help, it's important to not get hung up on the fact that you don't have anything to give people right now. Maybe you will down the road, or maybe you'll give back without even knowing it. Maybe the questions you ask or the help you're looking for prompts them to look at their career or business in a different way and perhaps that new perspective will help them with their own work or career.

Integrity, Intention, and Authenticity

When it comes to developing successful business relationships, I believe that there are three key factors. You want to pursue these relationships with integrity, and in ways that are intentional and authentic for you. It's important for all of us to be natural, but still be focused and committed to a clear purpose. It's a fine balance and it can be achieved. Let's break it down a little more to see how.

Integrity

This one is simple. Having integrity means being trustworthy and transparent. Let the person know your intention up front and be forthcoming about what you're interested in or what you need help with. Honor the other person's wants and needs as much as your own. Recognize that they have a legitimate choice to not help you at this particular time, for whatever reason.

Intention

Having intention is thinking through who you'd like to establish a relationship with and knowing what you want from that relationship. It's having an end result in mind when you call or walk in to see them, that you can easily communicate and one so you can both get the most out of your time together.

Authenticity

Authenticity means being true to yourself, of course, but also appearing to be exactly who you are and having your thoughts, words, and actions sync up naturally. You are being authentic when the way you appear to others is aligned with your intentions regarding them.

In short, having integrity, intention, and authenticity is about being yourself when you initiate and cultivate relationships.

Six Degrees of Separation

Strategic relationships are not just one-on-one; in a way they're network-to-network, and understanding this should provide extra motivation for pursuing them.

By network-to-network, I mean that when you connect with a person, you are also connecting within their entire network, and vice versa. When you understand this, it's easy to see how a little proactive networking will open all sorts of doors in ways you never anticipated.

Everyone has a network, so it's always worthwhile to ask a person you're talking with if they can suggest anyone else for you to talk with for help or a different perspective on whatever it is you've been talking about. You're expanding your network by asking someone to be a connector for you. But it works both ways and this is where you can reciprocate. Even if you don't think you have insights or expertise the other person will need, consider all the people in your network who could be valuable resources for others in all kinds of situations.

Just remember that sharing networks is like buying rounds on Wednesday beer night. If you always take but never offer, sooner or later people will notice your stinginess and their own generosity will dry up.

What Does Your Strategic Network Look Like?

It's time to take a look at your relationships or networks.

When I ask people to identify their strategic network, they often pull out their company's organization chart. This is a good place to start, but it can be limiting—a web of relationships should include your immediate line of reports and colleagues up and down the organization, but also across and out. This is a good time for women to think broadly and big.

It can help to stop thinking of your company as a traditional hierarchy and to think of it instead as a web of interconnected relationships that you can seek out and develop in multiple ways and at multiple levels.

Building Your Web: Sizing Up Your Network

Think about all the people who report to you, your peers, the executives in your organization, people outside of your organization such as contacts in your industry and at previous employers, and the business relationships you have within your community and social circle.

Try placing all these relationships in concentric circles based on how much day-to-day contact you have with them. Take a moment, and from the inside outward list the following:

- Relationships within your immediate team or functional area

- Contacts you have in your company but beyond your immediate team

- Customers and colleagues outside your company

- Friends and acquaintances who are also potential or current business connections

Your Network

Once you've completed your diagram, answer the following questions.

- How big is it?

- Which layers are bigger and which are smaller? Why?

- Is it balanced between internal and external people?

- Does it include people senior to you as well as peers and direct reports?

- Is it diverse by age, gender, nationality, race, industry, geography, etc.?

- Does it include long-term, short-term, and new relationships?

- How have most of these relationships developed?

- Is there a circle that should be bigger? Why is it underdeveloped?

Striking the Right Balance

Let's focus on one of the above questions for a moment. Specifically, how many of your relationships are within your company versus beyond it? Research shows that successful women split their time evenly between cultivating relationships inside and outside of their organization. How close do you come to this ideal, and on which side do you need to invest more time?

There may be times when you need more internal verses external relationships. This can depend on several areas; what your goals are, what you have coming up that you may need help on, current and future needs regarding knowledge and experience, etc. When considering the right balance consider the following questions.

Based on what you are focusing on in your job and in terms of your career development, what are some ways you can expand the part of your network that is smaller and correct that imbalance? Who are two or three people you might have seen from a distance or met in passing but have not taken the opportunity to talk with in a meaningful way? Perhaps in the next week you'll make a point of reaching out to one of those people and schedule a meeting.

The *Why* of Your Relationships

Next, start to think about what these relationships have that actually make up your strategic network. Consider, why do you maintain relationships with these particular people and why have you let other relationships dissolve away or fail to develop?

In particular, in terms of *your current job*, who of these people has helped you or could help you do the following?

- Improve your results
- Develop new skills
- Learn more
- Take a different perspective on business issues you deal with
- Identify or cultivate supporters for your important initiatives
- Mentor or develop others
- Form strategic alliances outside your organization
- Make your team more visible to key executives
- Provide support, encouragement, or advice when you need it
- Break through organizational barriers

These are all valid uses of your strategic relationships and you ought to have at least two or three people who can help you with each of them in this network!

In terms of your *career and/or professional growth*, who of these people has helped you or could help you with the following?

- Let people know who you are
- Clarify your career path
- Improve your opportunities for promotion
- Gain additional expertise you need to achieve your career goals

- Gain access to stretch projects that make you more visible in your company or industry
- Identify and groom a successor to you
- Stay abreast of market trends
- Share and celebrate your successes
- Act as a mentor when you need it

Your answers to these granular questions should help you answer these big-picture questions: How effectively are you using your existing network? And, what opportunities are you missing? How important are they to you?

Putting Your Web of Connections to Action

There are probably people in your network who you respect, who you know have been generally helpful to you, or people with whom you'd like to have a deeper relationship. Take it to the next level and think really *strategically* about those folks.

For some help, take a look at Table 6-1, Growing Your Strategic Network.

Start with the first column, Sphere of Relationship. This breaks down your life into three basic areas: your job, your career, and your extracurricular life—for example, your involvement with professional groups, not-for-profits, community organizations, or church.

Now look across the column headings and attack each sphere in four steps.

Areas of Focus: My number one rule is to have a goal before you decide who to engage with. In each sphere, jot down the top priorities or goals you are focusing on right now. For example, at work you might be trying to get a new project off the ground, whereas in your career, you're thinking about how to position yourself for your

Table 6-1 *Growing Your Strategic Network*

Sphere of Relationship	Who?	Value in Cultivating and Sustaining These Relationships	Commitments and Specific Actions (and Deadline)
Current Role Areas of Focus?			
Career/Personal Development Areas of Focus?			
Outside of Your Organization Areas of Focus?			

next promotion. Outside of work, you might be involved in recruiting a new director for a nonprofit board you sit on.

Who: Identify two or three people who are in your network, or who should be in your network, who would be potentially helpful to you in moving closer to that goal.

Value in Cultivating and Sustaining These Relationships: This is where you get granular. Articulate to yourself how specifically you believe each person might add value to the sphere where you've placed them. And don't forget to think of each one as a two-way relationship. Why might you be important to each of these people? And, how can you both benefit from establishing or furthering a relationship?

Commitments and Specific Actions: Take some thoughtful time to complete this column. Identify a concrete strategy for engaging each person. If you've done a good job of analyzing your personal links to these people and the mutual benefit to each of you, this part will be easier, so don't be afraid to go back and rethink the previous columns if necessary. Consider which relationships take priority based on the timeframes you have in mind for your goals in column one. And be realistic about how quickly you'll be able to concentrate on each relationship. It might be this week, the next three weeks, or by the end of the year.

Hint: Try to put one person on the list who will be a stretch for you; that is, a little out of your comfort zone.

And if there is someone on the chart who you've lost touch with, send an e-mail, pick up the phone, or drop a note saying something recently made you think of them and you'd love to catch up. If you happened to have read an article or come across a Web site you thought they might like, send it along as a show of good faith.

Success: How will you know that you've been successful? The answer is: When you routinely (perhaps not daily but reasonably often), and without thinking much about it, pick up the phone or meet with others for support, feedback, and advice. And when you also find yourself fielding those calls and meetings from others.

Seeking the Kindness of Strangers

I've talked a lot in this chapter about bringing new people into your network. I know this can be the most challenging part because you're going into it knowing that you want something from someone who might not even know you yet (at least not well).

Find a mutual acquaintance who can introduce you, if possible. But if not, don't let that deter you. Either way, being prepared is the best antidote to jangling nerves. Here's a list of questions to help you prep before you contact the person:

- What would you like to know from them?
- What would you like them to know about you?
- What do you have to offer them?
- What requests would you like to make?
- How formal would you like the relationship to be?
- For how long might you expect to sustain the relationship?

It also helps to play to your strengths. If you're an introvert, you may want to approach a person first by e-mail to introduce yourself and explain your request. If you're an extrovert, you might just pick up the phone and call or go to a function where there's a good chance you'll run into them. Understanding yourself and how you operate keeps you in that zone where you can remain authentic to yourself.

Follow up: One of the best ways to show your gratitude for help or advice is to follow up. A thank-you call or note immediately afterward goes without saying. But additionally, let them know how it turned out so they know you valued their advice and followed through on it. Beyond being polite, it makes you look professional and thorough. And it signals to the other person that you're interested in still being in touch with them. Besides, people appreciate knowing they were helpful.

Asking for Help

Let's talk about the *sticky floor* within this *sticky floor*: asking for help.

It's a challenging thing for people who view themselves as smart and capable to have to ask for help. They don't enjoy feeling incapable or at a disadvantage or vulnerable, and needing help can infer any or all of those things. And most people don't like putting others out of their way.

Women can be especially wary about saying those four little words, "can you help me?" at work, because they worry about being written off as not competent or confident enough in what they do. When I urge the women I work with to ask for help when they need it, they say that they worry they'll get shut down, or not taken seriously afterward, or even that they might get the wrong information.

Sometimes they've asked for help in the past, but didn't do a good job of thinking through who the right person would be to seek out or how to make the request, and as a result they got a disappointing response that discouraged them from trying it again. If you really do work with the advice and tools you've read about here, you'll develop a better feel for who to seek out on specific kinds of issues and how to approach them in a productive way.

I had a good lesson in the value of asking for help in my first job at General Motors. I knew nothing about manufacturing cars, managing production lines, or dealing with unions and shop stewards. Also as I mentioned earlier, I was the only woman on the shop room floor and not entirely welcome. I found myself managing production and labor relations among people who would have been happy to see me fail, and a few of them weren't above setting me up to fail. Of course, this was not exactly how GM described the job when they were recruiting me on campus at Purdue University. Lucky for me there was a person on the floor named Larry, who was in charge of quality control and parts.

When I first introduced myself to Larry, he was quite skeptical. "What's a girl like you doing in a place like this?" he asked by way of introduction. But at the very least, he wasn't openly hostile to having me as a boss. And he was instrumental in determining whether my line would be shut down or would run successfully on any given day. So I latched onto him, taking the time to get to know him and letting him know I appreciated the good job he was doing. I also put in many late-night hours learning the business so he could legitimately respect me.

I knew my investment had paid off when he came to me at 6:45 a.m. (just before my line was ready to start) one morning and said that we had a problem. Someone had sabotaged my line so we would not be able to get it up and running. The parts that were set to start going down the line at 7 a.m. were for another assembly line and were somehow moved to my line, a development that would have created mass confusion and major quality issues—an expensive mistake to say the least. Clearly this wasn't an innocent mistake—someone had really set me up to fail, even if all they intended was to get a few laughs out of it. I felt vulnerable, so I swallowed my pride and asked Larry, who was in charge of the parts going down the line, what he thought had happened. He told me, "I think someone is playing games with you and it's not right, so let me see what happened here."

Larry began to ask around and managed to identify the culprit, Bob, the superintendent. I reached out to Bob, we had a frank discussion and I was able to persuade him that it would be a bad idea to try that again. If I hadn't been able to admit I was in a jam, I would have had an expensive disaster on my hands. By not trying to do it all myself, I avoided an embarrassing moment and saved my career from an early derailment.

Don't Wait Until You Need a Relationship to Start It!

The incident with Larry also demonstrated to me the value of cultivating a relationship before you really need it. Larry knew I respected and trusted him. If he didn't, he might not have stuck his own neck out by bringing the problem to my attention. And if he didn't respect and trust me, he might not have helped me with it so readily.

It's easy to get bogged down with just getting the everyday work done, but this restricts your view. You get entirely caught up in the short term and forget to spend any time on your long-term goals, future challenges, or opportunities. Operating this way also curtails your network. You may keep in contact with the people who are important to the here and now, and let all others fall by the wayside. But if you wait to reach out at the time you need something, then you send a message that you're not good at relationship building and you *can* make people feel that they are being taken advantage of.

Having strong relationships that are strategic can bring so much value to people's life and work. With the right relationships, you can do just about anything you set out to do and in return can help others around you to do the same. It takes 18 months or more to develop a meaningful relationship—the kind of relationship where you can reach out and ask someone to be a key sponsor or a mentor.

Start today. If you usually eat lunch at your desk, or were planning to bring this book down to the company cafeteria, don't. Shoot an e-mail to a colleague you're overdue to check in with or are eager to know better and ask if they're free to grab a sandwich. You just don't know where it might lead.

Chapter 7

Capitalizing on Your Political Savvy

What Is Political Savvy and Why Do You Need It?

Anyone who has spent more than a few years in a corporate job knows that in any organization there are always going to be competing interests. And oftentimes, key people don't particularly want to admit that this is going on. In fact, given the collaborative team dynamics organizations are supposed to value today, executives and managers are less likely than ever to admit that politics happen.

But politics are always a factor and are an important element in most organizations—in ways both good and bad. Situations come up every day where you need to have critical information if you are going to be effective and achieve the results you want within your organization. The only way you're going to get what you need all the time is to be both politically and socially savvy. Or, to put it another way, you have to have the right radar so you can know what's coming and prepare for it.

Remember the chapter on self-awareness? In it, I talked about emotional intelligence, that cultivated internal awareness of the impact you have on others that helps you to manage your relationships.

This chapter, in contrast, is about the external awareness women need to focus on regarding their organization and its players. Some say that being politically savvy is like reading the tea leaves. Maybe so. It's certainly not always straightforward and it's never found in an employee handbook. But, for sure, the people most adept at leaf-reading are the ones who get promoted, are recognized for their hard work, and are most likely to achieve their personal and organizational goals.

Many women are not sure how to grasp this concept and some are reluctant to be political because they associate politics with people who are controlling, self-serving, dishonest, or even fake. But actually, the opposite is true. Gerald Ferris, a management and psychology professor at Florida State University says, "What sets apart a leader who is politically skilled from one who isn't is that the former can skillfully execute behaviors that are associated with politics and perceived as genuine, authentic, straightforward, and effective." Gerald says that, "Leaders who are not politically skilled are those most often seen as manipulative or self-serving."

Often women are reluctant to be political because early in their career they saw someone, probably a manager who had a direct impact on their work, use his or her political power in a way that spurred distrust or that had a negative effect on the people around them. Certainly there are people who use their political power for their own benefit, but this approach seldom works in the long term and sometimes backfires even in the short term. In contrast, to have ethical political savvy is to operate in a way that achieves the right business results for the organization, its people, and for you. If you apply your political savvy this way, you will always be able to offer a great value proposition for how you fit into the organization.

Good, ethical political savvy boils down to a few things: always having sources of reliable information so that you are ahead and on top of coming changes instead of chasing after them. It means disseminating information that makes you visible and garners the support you need for your initiatives. And it means knowing who your go-to people are for hearing the latest inside scoop and talking up the information you want disseminated.

People who are politically savvy have a few things in common. They:

- Know where to get the right information
- Understand what people want to know . . . and what they *don't* want to know!
- Know how to rally support for their agenda
- Are able to build bridges between their own and other people's best interests
- Are able to "read between the lines," which means knowing what people are really saying or feeling
- Know how to anticipate resistance in the organization and prepare to address it proactively
- Know what's going to happen before others do so they can refocus the right priorities at the right time and with the right people.

All this, done with the right intention, makes a person politically savvy. If this is a daunting concept, don't worry. You're not alone. The questions I am asked most frequently on the topic of political savvy are as follows:

- How do I know if I have it?
- How can I better understand the political dynamics in my organization?
- How do I figure out how information is really shared and how do I get access to the right information when I need it?
- How do I know if I'm picking up on the unwritten rules or social cues in meetings and other conversations?

- How do I recognize my own political blind spots before they become an obstacle or landmine for me?

This chapter will address these questions one by one.

How Do You Know When You Have It?

I usually answer this question with a set of additional questions. See how you would answer them.

Are You Politically Savvy?	Yes	No
1. Are you sought after as a key resource for information in your area of expertise? Do people expect that you will know before they do?		
2. Do you know how important decisions are made and by whom, in most cases? Do you know who most influences the decision-makers?		
3. Do you, in general, understand why and how things happen the way they do? Are you usually not surprised by events or announcements?		
4. Do you know, at any given time, who the key players are? Do you know who's in and who's out and why?		
5. Do you always trust that people mean what they say? Can you read between the lines in e-mails, meetings or even in general conversations?		

	Yes	No
6. Do you know when to speak and when to listen? Do you present your thoughts and opinions when others are ready to hear them?		
7. Do you have an executive presence? Do people see you as a leader? Do they recognize your value as well as your potential?		
8. Are people drawn to you? Do they seek you out and feel a connection to you? Do they want to spend time with you?		

If you answered a ubiquitous *yes,* then you can skip ahead, but if you've got at least one *no* up there, then this chapter will be worth your while.

How Do You Know When You Don't Have It?

Let me give you a great case study.

Sarah was a fast-track leader on her way to the executive suite when she hit a bump in the road. She and her team had spent months doing extensive research on a new and innovative product line for her business unit. She was responsible for setting the agenda and presenting the proposal to her executive team at an important meeting. On the day of the meeting, she sat at the table ready to go with her PowerPoint slides and key talking points in front of her. She had barely made a few opening remarks when she was barraged with questions that took her off course and away from her agenda.

This is how Sarah learned that the executive team had its own agenda. All she could do was sit and watch as they proceeded to take the meeting in another direction, using an idea that someone had thrown on the table impromptu. Sarah was in effect downshifted from meeting leader to meeting participant and she made the situation worse by personalizing it, becoming quiet, and showing her frustration.

What Went Wrong?

Let's take a look at how Sarah veered off course.

Unfortunately, Sarah had no idea that there was a predetermined political agenda for her meeting that had nothing to do with her plans. Why didn't this come up on her radar? She was an authority in her department and had a group of female colleagues she hung out with, but she hadn't made herself part of an informal network of the key stakeholders. So she didn't know that some of the company's key players had been talking for weeks about different products, and those informal conversations unofficially set the meeting agenda. Since she wasn't in on those conversations, she had no opportunity to informally let people know about her plans and to build support for them. So she walked into the meeting ill-informed and with no one in her corner.

But to make matters worse, Sarah also lacked the right presence. She should have taken back control of the meeting. Her proposal was supposed to be the basis for the majority of the meeting. But she failed to read the room. Sarah was so engaged in making her points that she failed to look around the table, read the faces of the key players, and observe the direction they wanted to take. Hence, she lost her bearings and her ideas crashed—without regard for how good or bad they might have been.

This is just one example of that old adage: Success is less about what you know and more about having the ability to connect with people. It's all about socializing your ideas, getting people to cooperate with you, and building bridges to meet others halfway.

Social Intelligence

A key component of political astuteness is something I refer to as *social intelligence*—the ability to get people to like, respect, and cooperate with you. It comes more naturally to some people than others, but for everyone it is to some extent an acquired art. It's the ability to be aware of what's going on around you, and to read, adapt, and engage with others in such a way that they want to align themselves with you. It comes into play during one-to-one conversations, while presenting to a key stakeholders' group (as we saw in the last case study), in handling difficult situations, or in seeking out the information from the right people to always be tapped into the big picture at your organization.

Social intelligence is a big part of what I'm talking about in this chapter, so I'm going to take some time to delve into it here. Below are four guidelines for cultivating your own social intelligence.

Learn How to Read Situations

Being able to walk into a room and instantly know what the dynamic is, who is influential, who you need to impress and steer clear of, and what everyone's individual and collective agendas are is something that heroes like Sherlock Holmes or Robert Ludlum's Jason Bourne can pull off. In the real world, people who seem to have this great radar are actually just people who have done their homework.

To have situational awareness you have to do the background work. Essentially, you have to take the time to get to know a person well enough that in any situation you can perceive their emotional state, their motivations, their willingness (or lack thereof) to interact, their intentions, and so on. You do this by having formal and informal conversations, reading e-mails, listening during meetings and off-the-cuff interactions, and taking in verbal and nonverbal cues.

Collectively these things tell you who in a particular situation has influence, who has credibility and clout, who has visibility, who is valued, and who is in a position of strength. They can also tell you who stands to win or lose in a situation and how that will determine their likely behavior based on their position, gender, age, etc.

Become Fluent in Nonverbal Cues

People often keep their most telling thoughts to themselves, especially when delivering criticism or bad news to a colleague or boss, or when they think their words won't have a meaningful impact. This is why it's important to learn to read nonverbal cues—body language—and meaningful silences that can be the first sign a situation is going wrong, or at least not as you planned.

Consider a woman I was coaching a few years ago who came to me with a situation at work that was troubling her, although she couldn't figure out why.

In a recent team meeting, she had to explain an upcoming project to her team. She shared that she had spent all weekend putting it together. She also explained that she knew it had an aggressive timetable that would require long hours, and then she asked for feedback. At first the room was pretty silent, she related. People eventually asked a few questions and mentioned a few conflicts with other deadlines but didn't raise as many issues or push back the way she thought they would. She decided she'd worried too much about getting their support. Afterward, no one said much to her about the project, but she noticed that one of the folks carrying the heaviest load on it had taken to eating at his desk rather than joining the group, so she assumed that this was why she wasn't getting updates on it the way she did with other projects.

One day she stopped by his desk to ask if he was having any problems and he said, "You don't see me complaining, do you?" So, she decided he was okay. Still she felt she was in an awkward place. She wanted to know how the project was coming along, but she didn't want to be a micro-manager. So she decided to just wait until the first milestone date to check in with him. After all, she figured, no news is good news, right?

Obviously she sensed that something wasn't right, or she wouldn't have come to me for feedback, but without more information she couldn't quite figure out what was bothering her. I told her that she needed to "read between the lines" of what was being said to her and look for what wasn't being said. In other words, are they avoiding looking at you when you speak or they speak to you? Are they tapping their fingers or pens on the table or just seem stressed or anxious when you talk about the project to them; shoulders held in, no smile or enthusiasm projected by their facial expressions, or just seem weary and tired? All of these are body language signals to look out for when reading between the lines.

Tune into Your Empathy

The idea that a high E.Q.—emotional quotient—can be more important than I.Q. gained mainstream currency in Daniel Goleman's best-selling book *Emotional Intelligence* (Bantam Books, 2006). This ability to relate to and connect with people is really just a way of adapting empathy to the workplace.

Empathy, of course, is pretty familiar to all of us. It generally means recognizing how someone feels and being able to put yourself in their place. At work, it might mean being attentive to others, adapting your language to your audience, making an effort to see others' points of view, asking insightful questions, and last but not least, listening actively.

One afternoon, I had to fly to one of Fairchild's operations in upper New York State for a meeting with our senior human resource team. As luck would have it, there was one other person on that flight, and it was our CEO. We both exchanged a few pleasantries, but beyond that I had no idea what else to say to him. But I had a flashback to my childhood and my entrepreneur father coming home from the office. One day I said to him, "You seem tired. How was your day?" He said, "You know, no one ever asks me how my day was." And he began to open up and talk about the frustrations and issues on the top of his mind. We connected in a new way and I began to understand and respect his many roles as a businessman.

So I asked my CEO what was on his plate these days and what was keeping him up at night? He smiled, and then to my surprise he shared some of his inner thoughts, hopes, and challenges. This connected us on a whole new level and hearing his perspective on the company encouraged me to talk to him about a major reorganization I was working on that he had a keen interest in—and I was able to present my side of the conversation in terms of his concerns and priorities.

This is still my way of connecting with people on their own ground—by asking questions, finding out where the other person is at that moment, and framing the conversation in a way I know they'll respond to.

Four Minutes

I once read that you either connect with a person or don't within the first four minutes of when you meet them. It only takes them that long to decide if they want to stay engaged with you or move on. Moreover, this is even true for people you know well! Here are a few tips for being instantly engaging:

1. Be *attentive* by focusing on the other person completely without distraction. I think that we forget the importance of doing this because we are so used to multitasking and dividing our attentions. But tuning out all but one thing for that period of time can be both challenging and rewarding.
2. Convey *appreciation* by saying something to the other person about what they've done or by doing something physical—a handshake or high-five is about right at the office. Sometimes it's as simple as a nod of the head, a note or e-mail of acknowledgment, or a mere "thank you."
3. Assert *affirmation*, which means to be true and express your level of understanding and commitment to others. Provide a response in a positive and supportive way.

Develop a Sense of Timing

Sometimes the best idea won't get heard because people are not ready to hear it. At other times, a person can hesitate to speak up to express interest in something or to raise a question and they lose an opportunity that never presents itself again.

Those nonverbal cues, your empathy, and awareness of context will give you a good idea of whether it's in your best interest to plunge ahead or hang back and wait for another day to speak.

For example, let's say you are presenting to your company's executive committee, and you introduce what you believe is a great idea but get no response—nothing either positive or negative. Are people looking out the window, chatting with each other, and checking their e-mail? Clearly you aren't grabbing them.

Before you press on, consider that maybe a major problem has occurred that you don't know about that makes your idea a lower priority or not entirely relevant anymore. Maybe the senior executives have a more pressing issue and you're keeping them from getting to it. Or, maybe it's a beautiful day and half the room is itching to get on the golf course and hit a round.

This is the time to pause, step back, and try to figure out what's going on to the extent that you can. If you think it's okay to press on with a different tack, say by asking questions and leading a discussion rather than talking, then press on. But if you sense that, for whatever reason, the room isn't with you today and isn't going to be, you might actually win a few points by suggesting that you table this idea for another time and asking what the group would prefer you do.

The same thing is true for voicing your opinion, asking for support, and providing help to others or checking in on them. If you aren't sure your timing is right, it's okay to ask a "couching question."

- **Before you spout an opinion:** Are you looking for feedback at this point or are you not quite ready for that yet?
- **Before asking for support:** How is everyone else's workload? Or, I'd like some help on this, when's a good time to talk?
- **Before offering unsolicited help:** How's the project going? Do you have any questions so far?
- **Before checking up on a team member:** I'd love an update on that project. When would be good for you?

What's Next

Cultivating your social intelligence is only a part—though a big part—of being more politically savvy.

But getting better at those things will sharpen your radar and your knack for both talking and listening to people, which will make it that much easier to play your political card well all the time.

Next, we're going to look at ways to build on and use those skills that will make you a mover and shaker on par with Nancy Pelosi, who politicked her way into the coveted speaker's chair in Congress.

Make Room for Informal Interactions

Work doesn't only get done inside the office, during formal sit-down meetings. In fact, I've found that some of the most important exchanges I've had with my bosses, clients, and peers have happened in passing, over a sandwich, an after-work drink, or between tee-offs on the golf course. Women who believe work is supposed to be all about work—as I once did—miss out on those small but important moments.

I'll give you an example: When I worked at Fairchild Industries, my boss, Bob, loved to go out for lunch, and I didn't. The job I had was a huge jump from my last one, so I felt that I needed every free moment I had to read up, write, or plan for what I had to do next—plus I have never been a big lunch eater. But Bob would call me at least twice a week and ask me to go out to lunch either with him or the guys. Eventually, I realized that I couldn't keep turning down my boss for lunch; it wasn't a great way to foster our relationship.

So, we "did lunch." And before the sandwiches were served, I realized that doing lunch was not the waste of time I had always assumed it was. Quite the opposite, it was a singular opportunity to learn important things that were subtle in nature, but as important as my day-to-day work.

After only a few of these exchanges I realized that, without lunch with Bob, my job would be much harder. Fairchild's CEO joined us one day. While he would never have asked me to lunch on my own—

I wasn't at quite that level—getting to tag along with Bob, who *was* at that level, was a fabulous opportunity. Over soup, I learned what was on the CEO's mind, what his priorities were, where the company was heading and, by inference, what he viewed as the top priorities for the human resources, and how I could better support the organization. I came back to my office with information I could use to prioritize my work to make the best impression on the people above me.

In general, my many lunches with Bob and others put me in with the in-crowd. I gained a lot of important information I never would have had otherwise that helped me to understand how the company worked and how key players made decisions. It's the information that I most credit with making my time at the company successful.

Get Good at the Prep Work

Think of the most polished female leaders you know: maybe Avon CEO Andrea Jung, Hillary Clinton, or Oprah Winfrey. Their nails and hair are always styled, they think carefully about what they wear to every meeting, social event, and public appearance. They anticipate the questions people will ask them and think very carefully about what they say and how they say it whenever anyone outside of their innermost circle is in earshot. They're always on-message. In short, they're well put together. They project presence and a carefully thought-out image. They know what they want to say and what they do and don't want people to know about them. People respond to this polish and it's what enables them to get things done.

Clearly you don't have the advisers, assistants, and interns they do to help them keep themselves so well put-together, but the idea is still there. Women who are priming themselves for the executive suite work at presenting themselves well. They don't have chipped nails, they make time for a good haircut, and they always sound and look the part of a leader who is in control of her game. This allows them to move easily and confidently among the people they need to know to do their jobs well.

Like other things in this chapter, this great public face might come more easily to some than others, but the best way to make a good impression is to do the right prep work. The rest of this chapter talks about the most politically savvy way to present yourself to others—and the homework you'll need to do it.

Executive Presence—Locate Yours

The starting point for all this prep work is in your sense of presence.

Executive presence is one of those things that we know when we see it. Someone who has it stands out in a crowd, gets noticed in a positive way, and garners respect.

Presence is a component of political savvy because with a strong sense of presence you have an increased ability to have your messages resonate with others, and when you resonate, you connect. When you connect, you can engage others in what you want to say, what you want them to understand or learn, and even what you want them to do.

To assess your *executive presence*, take the following assessment that I often use with women when I speak at numerous Senior Women's Leadership Forums.

Step 1: Imagine a new colleague has just met you and has spent an hour working with you. Write down how you think that person would describe you. Try to come up with seven or eight characteristics.

Step 2: Think about how you would *like* them to describe you and write down those characteristics, too.

Step 3: Compare how others would actually perceive you against how you would like them to.

Step 4: Don't sweat the results too much. During one session, a participant came up with this list of ideals: collaborative, caring, passionate, genuine, trustworthy, witty, reliable, honest, and engaging. These are all powerful descriptors and they indicate what this woman wanted her presence to be. You might want to write off such a list as unrealistic, but that doesn't really matter. What matters is that she aspired to being viewed this way. Working toward these ideals enabled her to view herself this way and boost her confidence, and believe it or not, this subtle shift was enough to get her more of the positive attention and respect she was seeking.

Whatever your ideal characteristics are, work on seeing yourself in those terms and asserting that side of you, and you'll see a change in how you react to things and how people react to you.

The Nine Elements of Executive Presence

Many women come to our WILL program to develop their executive presence. We have a set of nine characteristics that we think are usually associated with executive presence. They're listed below. Size them up and see how many you have and where you fall short. No one will have all of them without a little work. But cultivating these traits is something that you can work on with a career coach or in a leadership-training workshop.

- **Candor**: being honest and telling it like it is

- **Clarity:** telling your story in a compelling way

- **Openness:** being willing to consider another's point of view

- **Passion:** expressing yourself in a way that shows you really believe in something

- **Poise:** remaining centered, calm, and handling yourself well in all situations

- **Self-confidence:** having a demeanor of assurance in what you say and do

- **Sincerity:** believing in and meaning what you say

- **Thoughtfulness:** thinking through something before you speak

- **Warmth:** being accessible to others and interested in them

Market Yourself

Some call it tooting your own horn, but the fact is there's nothing wrong with that. Part of doing a good job is hitting your performance targets *and* taking credit for them. But you don't have to develop a hard-hitting salesperson's personality if you don't have one. Marketing your value and leadership across the organization just means letting people know who you are, what you've done, and what you can do. Prepping for it requires knowing your value and learning to share it with the right people, at the right time, and for the right reasons.

Many women I talk to assume that meeting their goals and getting the results their boss wants will get them the credit they deserve. But don't assume people know anything about you that they don't hear about from you. This is true even if you are brilliant or you've achieved some major accomplishments. Why? People are moving at such a fast pace that they don't have any more time than you do to proactively look into other people's pasts and their accomplishments. Even if the person hired you and has read your resume (and talked it over with you), it doesn't mean all your abilities and experiences remain top of mind to them. When something you've done previously—even a few months ago—becomes relevant, it's important and up to you to remind others about it.

It's easy to think that no one wants to hear you talk about yourself (and yes, there are people who do it way too much), but I find that people are curious beings and want to hear about the accomplishments, stories, and unique qualities of others. Moreover, it's always better to take opportunities to let people know what you care about, what you are good at, and how your strengths and experience can help them along the way, than to let them make uninformed assumptions about you.

Kathleen Matthews, a senior executive at Marriott International, says, "If you want credit for what you do, you need to let others know about it." Kathleen says you can't work in a cave as a leader. You need to communicate what you learn, whom you know, and what value you can bring to others. She also says that opportunities to do that don't always just fall in your lap. You need to proactively seek out opportunities to be seen and heard and make your abilities known. Above all, she says, don't underplay *you*—false modesty has no place in the executive suite.

Consider this: I gave a talk in Washington, D.C., to a round-table of 20 up-and-coming women. No one knew each other and so I asked them to introduce themselves and to share one thing they were very proud of at that particular time in their life. Eighteen of them mentioned something about their children, while only two gave a work-related or personal example. Now, I realize that we are proud of our children, but I couldn't help but detect false modesty in the air. These women felt that bragging about their children was somehow safer and more socially acceptable than talking about themselves. But here was an opportunity for them to network and to share something that might catch someone's interest for all sorts of reasons and lead to a great new professional relationship. It was a missed opportunity to market themselves.

A number of years ago, I got thrown into a dinner forum where the diners were all men. A friend drove me home and he said, "You didn't say anything. Were you feeling okay?" I said that I really felt as though I couldn't add anything of interest to the conversation—all they talked about was sports, business, and their last golf game. My friend then said to me, "Becky, you can talk with anybody and fit in . . . you just need to think ahead sometimes and plan what you might say early on." He said, "Next time, think about what kinds of issues you think people will be interested in—what kinds of questions would you ask them? Think of questions that may stretch their opinions or get them curious. Or even better yet—tell a short and memorable story." My friend then said, "Don't be shy, tell them you are president of a well-known leadership development organization. Let them know in the first thirty seconds some of the premier clients you have and tell about an interesting project your company just worked on."

To my friend's point, it is all about sharing your uniqueness and speaking with a sense of passion and enthusiasm. Find the uniqueness in what you are doing and link it to what they want to do. Everyone will be tuned in and will want to learn more. Humans are curious people and generally, if thought through, they are genuinely interested in hearing who you are and what you do. Also, I find that once you do it the first time it gets easier every time.

A Natural Way to Market Yourself

Marketing yourself isn't something you always have to set out to do in a bold, proactive way. There are other ways to market yourself that might seem subtler and come more naturally to you.

For example, say you've been invited to a meeting of people from different departments and you're all there to share advice and expertise. If a problem or question comes up that's familiar to you, this is your chance—by all means, let the others know you went through something similar and this is how you handled it, why you were successful, and what you learned that might be applicable here. People like to learn from other people's challenges and failures. Sharing stories is a natural way to let people know what you have done and to show you can relate to their situation. And people remember stories and anecdotes more than they remember you telling them you're good at one thing or another. Additionally, telling your own story signals that you're confident enough in yourself to be open and put yourself out there. That puts people at ease around you.

There are opportunities to share information about yourself this way every day in meetings, watercooler conversations, and informal situations. So keep your eyes open for them and speak up!

My Favorite Marketing Tool—The Elevator Speech

Think of any consumer product you like—cars, toothpaste, snack crackers—and imagine all of the things the manufacturer wants you to know about them. A snack cracker might come in a variety of unique flavors, have health benefits, and have better taste and texture than the competition. But in a 30-second TV commercial they don't tell you the life story of the cracker; they boil their message down to the most essential things that will create an overall impression about the cracker and hopefully pique your interest in learning more (or trying them!).

That's you. Every day, in business meetings, at client lunches, at cocktail parties, or in the stands at pee-wee soccer games, we all get asked what we do. How often do you sigh to yourself and think *where to begin?* You might just offer up your title, which probably doesn't mean much to anyone outside your company, or you fumble through a lengthy, jargon-filled explanation that serves as a conversation stopper. You can do better.

Next time you're stuck in traffic or a waiting room or while you're taking a long shower, make use of the time and work on your personal TV commercial—otherwise known in business as your *elevator pitch*. Come up with a pithy, plain-English way to describe what you do in no more than two or three sentences. Try it out on a few people—your partner, your kids, your assistant, or your best friend—and see if they think it resonates. And when you've got it down, stick to it and pull it out like a verbal business card every time the question comes up.

Chic Thompson, a well-known speaker on creativity, a fellow at the Darden Business School, and the author of *What a Great Idea 2.0* (Sterling, 2007) knows that after lectures or speaking engagements or even just a party, people will wind up asking him about himself and his myriad of activities—speaking, teaching, writing, running a company—that make up his career. So he's a big believer in the elevator speech to pull it all together.

"It's all about letting people know how invaluable you really are," Chic says. "And you do that by letting people know your uniqueness. I always rehearse my introduction," Chic says. There was a time when even he struggled with his elevator speech. Then he started asking himself, what are the characteristics that make me unique. And before heading into an event, he thinks about which of those things will be most interesting to people in the context of that situation.

Sometimes he'll play up his day-to-day work. "I am an ex-Disney cartoonist and I help people to come up with creative solutions in their work. I have a passion for teaching and I am a teacher at Darden." Sometimes he will share that he's dyslexic, but that his training has helped him to think in opposites. At other times he'll say simply, "I've worked for Disney and the company that makes Gore-Tex, and I teach creativity." But it's variations on a common theme—he always tries to convey a sense of his uniqueness.

So before you enter into the next meeting, luncheon, holiday party, or you meet your CEO, literally, in the elevator, follow Chic's lead and refine your pitch, or TV commercial, to idiosyncrasies that make you *you*.

Practice Graceful Gratitude

One more suggestion: When you share about yourself and get a compliment in return, just say *thanks*! I've observed so many women who have developed the art of deflecting, playing down, or avoiding well-deserved compliments. Some women know they did a great job or were responsible for a major win for their organization and instead of accepting a compliment with an enthusiastic *thank you very much*, they say, "It would not have been possible without my team," or "It was no big deal—you could have done it too," or "Wow, do you really think so?" They panic at the idea of having the spotlight on them and in some cases try to turn it on someone else. I'm all for sharing the glory with the team, but don't ever diminish the value of your own contribution.

Life Needs Dress Rehearsals: The Meeting Before the Meeting

Just as you prep yourself for success by working on your personal message, it's important to prep your team and your key supporters so that when it's time for the real "show" to go on, you can be confident that you'll all be on the same message and you won't have any awkward surprises, like Sarah, who we met at the beginning of the chapter.

This sort of prep work plays out every day at all levels of the organization. The next time you're in a meeting and everyone readily embraces a new idea, ask around. Chances are the person leading the meeting held a series of pre-meetings to ensure she had ferreted out any obstacles or critical issues, discussed them openly with the people who raised them, and worked to build consensus before the idea was discussed publicly. They probably had just such a meeting with you.

I've spoken with several women who, like Sarah, were frustrated and demoralized after having presented a brilliant idea and not received the attention or recognition it and they deserved. They didn't practice politics by selling their idea and bringing people on board individually. You can do this one-on-one coalition building while walking between meetings, over lunch, on an airplane, on the golf course, or even in the gym! But trust that just as so-called backroom politics move cities and nations, they also impact everyday business situations.

Anne Altman, managing director, U.S. Federal IBM Corporation, told me that before she even considers trying to get people to buy into a new idea or proposal, she needs to understand that the company supports her at many levels. She believes you need to build support person by person before presenting to the larger organization. "This requires a considerable investment of your time up front," Anne says. But she has found firsthand that it's the only way to really get things done.

She gives this example from her own experience:

Several years ago, Anne decided to launch a major change effort to assess and adjust her organization's compensation plan. This was a tough task because it required asking for more money. She began by thinking about things that could derail her proposal and where she would encounter resistance. Then, she developed a plan and made sure to include a discussion for how it would benefit not just her organization, but also all of IBM. As she was developing her proposal, she talked with key stakeholders above her and outside of her group to understand their views, concerns, and needs. As a result, she was able to articulate a broader vision in the presentation she eventually gave. Anne also astutely identified one or two people that she knew would support her in the meeting where she planned to make her presentation. These were people she knew would see the benefit of the proposed compensation plan and who would talk about the advantages of it to others. Anne knew that she would need support in the meeting and that she couldn't rely on it without first presenting the idea to would-be supporters, and addressing their questions and concerns. The whole process gave her the coalition she needed, but it also gave her a broader perspective and new ideas that made her presentation stronger and more likely to appeal to more people.

Sure this takes time, and people groan about endless meetings before meetings. But look at our two case studies, Sarah and Anne. Both put time and effort into their presentations in different ways—one focused on honing her pitch, the other on marketing it. You have to ask yourself, in the end, who made better use of her time and effort? More important, which of these women do you see reaching the executive suite?

Chapter 8

Making Your Words Count

The Art of Conversation—Something Worth Talking About

Your credibility and power as a leader depends greatly on how others perceive you. And since how well you communicate greatly impacts that perception of you, it's probably true that *you are what you say and how you say it*. So, making your words count—ensuring that you get the attention and respect you desire and deserve when you speak— is ultimately critical to your success. The image you convey with every aspect of your communication will help or hinder your ability to influence people, impact decisions, and will play a major role in determining whether or not you are invited into the higher ranks that lead to the executive suite.

Now, it might seem that this should be easy for us to do well because communication is a skill we use every hour of every day. Much research supports my personal experience that as leaders and executives, we spend close to 80 percent of our day communicating. Unfortunately, I think because we use our communication skills so continuously, we take them for granted and don't work to develop them after we begin to achieve success in an organization. So, it's no wonder that (combined with the statistic I heard recently that 60 percent of all communications at work are misconstrued anyway!) we aren't as effective in communicating as we'd like to be.

This chapter talks about how and why we as women might limit our overall communications capacity and effectiveness, and it provides 10 guidelines for *making your words count.*

How Can You Make Your Words Count?

SHAMBAUGH'S WILL program and our Executive Coaches help women leaders enhance and capitalize on their communication skills. The first step in this process is having them assess themselves across a full spectrum of skills and techniques. Surprisingly, we often find that there are some aspects of communication that women are less aware of and some simple but powerful techniques that they haven't considered using.

To explore how well you do in these key areas of communication, take a moment to answer *yes* or *no* to the following questions.

Making Your Words Count	Yes	No
1. My voice and speaking pattern make it easy for people to understand me.		
2. I adapt my communication style to achieve key outcomes or ensure people hear what I say.		
3. I balance making key points with sharing details.		
4. I actively listen by paraphrasing, summarizing, asking open-ended questions, and showing interest in what people are saying.		

	Yes	No
5. I speak up when I think I have something to say even when there is controversy or I am the only woman in the room.		
6. I avoid going into too much detail when I explain things.		
7. I explain factual information clearly and simply.		
8. I plan what I am going to say and how I am going to say it.		
9. I use my body language to capitalize on my communications.		
10. Instead of speaking, I focus on drawing out other people's ideas and perspectives in meetings or conversations.		

Did you say *no* to any of these questions? Rarely does anyone master all of these areas, but just by taking this quick assessment, it should be clear that being a good communicator is a multidimensional competency. Everyone has natural strengths in some areas as well as opportunities for improvement in others. The key is to learn to use the full suite of communication skills and techniques, and to adapt them to the situation, audience, and goal at hand.

The Three Elements of Successful Conversation

Let me start by mentioning that three factors reliably determine the success of any conversation. First, to many people's surprise, nonverbal language constitutes 55 percent of the overall message a person conveys while speaking. These signals include body language, such as how you sit in a chair or at a table, and whether or not you appear to be actively listening and interested. Next comes voice, which accounts for 38 percent of a speaker's effectiveness. A person's inflection, tone, pauses between sentences and thoughts, and the speed at which a person talks make a strong impression and can dramatically alter the meaning and direction of a conversation. Finally, the words a person chooses to use, or not use, account for about 7 percent of her effectiveness. So, regardless of the topic a person is discussing or audience she is speaking with, the cadence of her voice and the image she conveys with those nonverbal cues matter just as much as what she's actually saying. Combine these three factors and cumulatively they make or break a person's ability to achieve the desired outcome for that conversation! So, making your words count is really all about *how you say it*!

Guidelines for Making Your Words Count

Below are 10 specific areas with ideas you can use immediately to start polishing your communication skills. These guidelines are intended to make you more aware of how you communicate and give you suggestions for increasing your overall effectiveness as a communicative leader. Pick and choose the ones that resonate with you!

Guideline 1: Capitalize on Nonverbal Communication

Have you ever talked to someone who didn't look you in the eye? How did that make you feel? Or maybe you have been in a conversation with someone who fidgeted while you were speaking and didn't seem especially interested in what you were saying. These are examples of nonverbal cues—body language, eye contact, and other subtle and not-so-subtle signals that tell you (better than anything coming out of a person's mouth!) how engaged or bored, confused or clear, or even recalcitrant a person is.

Body language—and its connection to "reading between the lines"—was mentioned in an earlier chapter. Hearing information and observing the corresponding body language helps us to pick up on what someone is really thinking and feeling. Turning inward, paying attention to your own body language, can help you to understand how you come across to others and help you communicate more effectively.

I once attended a board meeting where Sue, one of the board members, tried to speak up in an important discussion. Sue is a brilliant woman with a strong engineering background. While her words were well thought out and technically right, people were not engaged. Some were actually nodding off and others were making their action list for the week. I noticed that instead of looking at the people around the table and making eye contact, Sue had her head down. To make matters worse, she was sitting back in her chair. Sue is a small woman, so for many people in that room she literally was invisible. She was filling the room with words, but while her words were correct, she failed to use her body language to project the energy and confidence she needed to engage the people around her and bring her message home.

Recognizing and making good use of body language is one of the hardest communication skills to master, partially because it's the hardest to see and understand. We all get caught up in unconscious patterns or behaviors that are hard to recognize in ourselves and, therefore, hard to adapt. But the nonverbal cues, while subtle, are a big factor in whether we connect, influence, and assure the people we're talking to.

One way to learn how to use body language effectively is by observing the body language of others. Next time you are in a meeting or at a social engagement, look around and observe who conveys a sense of self-confidence through their body language. They usually make good eye contact, sit up straight—no slouching—greet people with a strong handshake, smile, and seem relaxed with who they are. To contrast, take note of people who appear less self-confident or powerful. They may have a weak handshake, keep their eyes downcast or roaming, slouch, or speak in a hesitant voice. All of these actions send signals across a room, and it only takes a few minutes for others to generate an impression from them.

Another good idea is to have a friend observe you in action communicating in meetings or making presentations, and give you feedback on your particular body language in those situations. Ask about your eye contact, posture, hand gestures, attentiveness, and enthusiasm. Be sure to ask for their ideas on what you do well along with what you do that might be getting in the way of you being perceived as a powerful and effective communicator.

Guideline 2: Become an Active Listener

Communication is always a two-way endeavor. It's important to learn to be a good listener and to demonstrate that you understand other people by paraphrasing or repeating what they say back to them in a different way, summarizing what you think their main points are, and using short prompts like- *Uh-huh, Really?,* or *I see,* as well as other supportive body language to convey your interest.

Ann Hackett, president of Horizon Consulting Group, LLC, says that listening is the best way to better understand your organization and what it does. People are often so eager to make a contribution at a meeting or in a conversation that they don't take time to listen and understand what is going on around them. They can easily misunderstand or underestimate the value a business is trying to create, what's on the minds of the people in the room, or the company's values and how they play out organizationally. As a result, poor listeners can run up against the corporate culture or end up being discounted because their comments reflect a lack of understanding of the issues at hand.

Listening also allows you to process what people are saying, and it allows you to integrate and connect the solutions that different people may not see because they are only focused on their own ideas. In other words, listening and taking in all the information at hand allows you to better see the big picture and communicate it back to the group.

Ann said, "I often see people play very powerful roles at a later point in a meeting because they were good listeners earlier. They have actually seen insights and are able to integrate things that can help move a meeting forward in a very powerful way."

Being a good listener sometimes calls for you to withhold your opinions or conclusions while you make your way through a series of conversations or meetings that together give you the entire picture of a situation—like a mystery detective talking to all the suspects and piecing together the whole story that no one else sees before drawing a conclusion and solving the case. This helps you to share your thoughts most appropriately—a critical aspect of making your words count.

Ann says that there are times she advises people to go into a meeting and say nothing, simply listen, and pay attention to what there is to learn. She explains, "When people participate from a place of listening and observing instead of speaking, they report back that they have learned far more about the dynamics, the power base, how decisions get made, and where the influence is. It puts people in a different place with different objectives."

We've always been taught that speaking up—raising our hand in class, so to speak—is the best way for us to show our confidence and demonstrate our ability. But, most of us can still work on better listening skills. Here are a few tips:

Tips for Listening

1. Be curious and open to others' views and perspectives.
2. Be patient. Avoid jumping in to be heard. Later on you might learn you were coming from the wrong perspective, which could discount your effectiveness.
3. Be a connecter. Build a bridge between diverse views and connect the dots into a whole solution.
4. Observe others to see if they are engaged, understand what you are saying, or are buying into it.
5. Don't pretend you are listening. That is a good way to lose the respect of others and even alienate them.
6. Listen with empathy and compassion so that you can detect the feelings, spirit, and energy from others on a certain topic or issue.
7. Pay attention to context. What is the experience or situation behind a person's point of view? What are that person's possible motives?
8. Paraphrase and summarize. Repeat what people say back to them in your own words to convey that you are fully engaged in the conversation and understand what they're telling you.
9. Assume the best. Believe that everyone has a positive contribution instead of ruling them out before hearing what they have to say. If you approach them with a positive intent, even a "difficult conversation" can become an opportunity to explore positive solutions.

Guideline 3: Plan Your Message

Imagine you're in a job interview or introducing an idea to an influential stakeholder or about to engage in a difficult conversation. The person you are talking to suddenly says that he has three minutes left before they have to run off to another meeting. Ugh! How do you make sure you have made enough impact to get to the outcome you want in such a short period of time?

Your instinct might be to jump in and start talking, hoping that your thoughts will keep up and you'll make sense. Resist it. Too many people jump into a conversation without thoughtful preparation or consideration of the key elements for success. Take 30 of your pressure seconds—or even 45—to organize your thoughts by asking yourself the following questions:

1. What result do I want to achieve?

2. What key points do I need to make?

3. How should I say it to get the result I want?

Addressing these questions, whether in the moment or before you begin any critical conversation, will help you communicate more powerfully and effectively in all situations. Once again, thinking about your intention and planning your message delivery will help you to bring the things you need most to the conversation and present them in the most effective way.

Guideline 4: Keep It Simple and Stay on Message

At WILL, we spend a lot of time focusing on communication. We have heard for years that women are masterful communicators, collaborators, and connectors, but they often fail to capitalize on this natural strength, limiting their effectiveness and diminishing their power and voice. Over time, I have actually observed that this is true. Why is this?

In *The Female Brain*, Dr. Louann Brizendine presents statistics that provide some answers. On average, women have 11 percent more neurons in their brains than men, and these are dedicated to emotions and communications. Louann says that our communication capacity is evidenced by the fact that we speak about 20,000 words per day, an average of 250 words per minute, while men average 7,000 words per day or 125 words per minute. With such a knack for gabbing, it would seem that women should have an advantage over men in terms of communicating in the workplace.

However, the number of words a woman speaks per day or minute is not the best way to measure her effectiveness. Communicating by giving lots of details, talking about how you feel, and trying to involve everyone in the conversation does not always lead to action or results as effectively as being direct and succinct. The people you talk to—just like you—are busy and their minds are already filled with information. *Less* is truly better.

Shakespeare noted in *Hamlet*, "brevity is the soul of wit." But being a woman of few words goes to the heart of being a good communicator in general. This is where our extraordinary capacity to speak—250 words per minute—is a hindrance. Our desire to share everything about how we got from point A to point Z is not necessarily what the listener wants to hear. Often a busy executive, or a direct report for that matter, just needs the bottom line. It's good to share details and to demonstrate your thought process, but it's just as important to self-edit and choose the most pertinent details to share.

A lasting and memorable example of keeping your communications simple is the Gettysburg Address. This speech, written by President Abraham Lincoln, lasted no more than about 10 minutes and was under 200 words. It left an imprint in people's minds for over 200 years. It brings to light how powerful and well crafted a simple message can be.

I learned early on how keeping your communications simple and to the point was important for getting people to do what you want them to do. I had a high school science teacher who had a brilliant mind. One day I stopped by his desk to ask about my homework assignment and got an hour-long lecture on the whole human anatomy. He was sharing great knowledge, but it wasn't what I wanted to know, and I tuned out after the first five minutes.

When you are an expert on a subject and feel passionate about it, it's easy to get carried away and go on for too long, alienating your listener instead of catching them up in your enthusiasm.

The antidote? When you are getting ready to speak or propose something to someone, just cut to the chase up front. Prioritize and give them your key points, then ask if they have any questions or want more detail about anything.

Rebecca Ranninger, chief human resources officer at Symantec, says that from an early age women are inclined to gather all the details they can about things in which they're interested. But then they use that same idea generation process when they are communicating with others, and want to share every little thing they know. Rebecca says you are sure to lose people if you start with, "Well this is how I got started . . ." Her advice is, "Start where you want to end up, and then work backwards. Your audience needs three good reasons why they should know something and why they should go there or do this," she says. "The further you go beyond the basics, the more opportunity you have to lose them."

Keeping it simple is also key when explaining a complex issue. Using acronyms or jargon might make you feel authoritative and like an "insider," but know your audience. What is convenient shorthand with one group will leave another clueless as to what you are talking about. Gerri Elliott, corporate vice-president of World Wide Pubic Sector of Microsoft, says, "I believe in simplicity in words and thoughts. In a company like Microsoft, it can be easy to overcomplicate things. For example, it can get very complicated to explain why and how Microsoft is shifting from being a product company to being a solutions company. There are many complex parts of this strategy to understand, but that does not mean we need to confuse, worry, or frustrate our employees. So I work really hard at simplifying my message." Gerri says, "My tip (to both men and women) is something very simple: Always write down your thoughts before you speak. Whether I have 20 minutes to connect with 20 or 20,000 people, I write down my thoughts and then read them out loud to myself. Doing this forces me to keep it simple." Gerri's technique helps her get focused on communicating the message she wants to get across and not get off track. On the other end, people remember things better if the speaker's points are packaged and organized in an easy and understandable way.

Here are some ideas for how to keep your communication simple and to the point:

1. Understand your audience. Talk about what is relevant to them and not just about what interests you. This will help you to focus on the *right* things.
2. Balance detail with emphasis on key points. What do people need and want to know to understand your message? How much detail is enough? Make your statement, then ask others if there is anything they want to know more about.
3. Stay on message. Make sure you open and close with your key message and make it easy to follow from one point to the next.
4. Organize and crystallize your message. Instead of thinking in terms of 50 or 500 words, think in terms of making three key points.
5. Speak concisely. Don't use five sentences when one will do.

6. Ask questions to learn what is foremost on people's minds, and then tailor your message that way.
7. Don't feel rushed. Take time to ask, listen, think, and then speak.

To be convincing in what you say, you need to own your message. One important way to do this is to stay on point throughout your conversation or presentation. Resist going off on side points that can distract people or dilute your message. And don't allow others to pull you off your message, either. If someone asks a tangential or utterly unrelated question, it's okay to say that you'd like to stick to the topic at hand, but that you'd be happy to answer their question afterward.

I think of it as planning my route to a destination. If it's Sunday afternoon and I'm interested in enjoying the countryside, I might pick a route that meanders and takes more time than usual. But if it's a weekday and I'm heading to a client's office, that's a different story. I pick the route that is most direct and least likely to present delays for roadwork or congestion, so I can minimize my chances of something going wrong.

Work on owning and staying on your message by following these key tips:

1. Lead with your key points.
2. Determine your goal. Are you telling or selling? *Telling* is understanding what others need to know. *Selling* is understanding what others need to know and feel.

> 3. Summarize your key points before ending your conversation. You can open up and be passionate about something as long as you always stick to your two or three main points and drive them home.

Guideline 5: Leverage the Use of Questions

We don't create ideas so much as we reveal great ideas by asking good questions.

—DR. JONAS SALK,
creator of the polio vaccine

Imagine this scenario: You have a 15-minute meeting and you need to make the most of it. How do you make sure you connect with the other person and talk about what's on your mind in a way that will engage them and win them to your point of view in that amount of time? One of the best ways might be to start with a question, or several questions. You can use questions to determine the person's position on the issue, establish a person's priorities for whatever it is you want to accomplish, and gain his or her interest in what you want to discuss.

For example, if you are talking with the CEO or your boss about a project you are working on, start the conversation by asking what their top concerns and top priorities are on the topic. This will help you to think about the issue from other angles. It will also help you to better understand what they are looking for and to channel your conversation in a direction that gives the other person exactly what he or she needs in order to be on your side.

Following are some other good techniques for asking questions that allow you to share your "best" point of view and build a bridge for a productive conversation with others:

1. Start with open-ended questions that encourage the other people to speak and to share what's on their mind. These questions often begin with what, how, and why: What is it that bothers you? How do you see that happening? Why is that important to you?
2. Use closed questions to clarify the information and validate your assumptions: When is this due? Are you okay with this project? When can we meet? Closed questions can be answered with a yes or no, or a single word or phrase response.
3. Summarize and then share your reaction and point of view. Make linkages and build a bridge back to what the other person said as much as possible.

Guideline 6: Adapt Your Style to Your Audience

Tweaking the golden rule just a little, *my* golden rule is, *do unto others as they want to be done unto.* It is not about saying things your way, but saying them in the best way for others to hear them. Your goal is to get to your desired outcome. To do that, get on the same wavelength of the person you are speaking with. It helps you to empathize with their point of view and helps them to relate to you, which increases the odds of the conversation yielding the result you want.

Back in the 1960s, Dr. David Merrill looked at people's social styles and developed a method that takes these styles into account to make each one of us a more effective communicator. His strategy is based on two dimensions of behavior: *assertiveness*, which takes into account how a person influences others (e.g., by asking questions or making statements), while *emotion* covers how a person expresses her feelings to others. He found that people generally have one of four styles:

- *The Driver:* Someone who likes you to get to the point quickly and doesn't want to hear all the details.
- *The Expressive:* Someone who wants to be noticed and likes to think out loud to generate new ideas.
- *The Amiable:* Someone who wants to get along and really cares about the feelings of the entire team.
- *The Analyst:* Someone who wants to get it right, wants all the facts before making a decision, and asks lots of questions.

Usually you can identify a person's preference of how he or she wants to be spoken to by just watching that person interact with others one-on-one or in a meeting. If a person seems to be down to business and bottom line, the worst thing you can do is spend a lot of time up front chatting or building rapport or giving too many details. Avoid the small talk and get to the point. You want to come well prepared for these situations and keep your conversation brief and focused. For those who are more open and have a more collaborative style, you may want to ask them personal questions up front or talk about their personal interests before jumping into the topic you are discussing.

I have found that understanding these styles can be useful for understanding the person I'm talking to and quickly assessing the best way to get my point across to him or her. Knowing these personality types will help you to follow *my* golden rule: *Do unto oth-*

ers as they want to be done unto and you'll be amazed how much easier it will be to make your words count!

Guideline 7: Pay Attention to Your Speaking Habits

So, umm, we all, over time, you know, pick up speaking habits that, umm, come out without our even realizing it, you know? And, umm, that can be a distraction in professional conversation, right? Umm, it really can, you know?

It's important to pay attention to your verbal tics and other distracting habits in order to learn to control them. Chris Hipwell, a sales executive at Pfizer, Inc., says, "We women sometimes aren't aware that our sentences go on and on. We have this knack for connecting and extending our thought process out loud by using such words as *and*, *but*, *because*, or *umm*." Chris says a large part of her job involves communicating with or presenting to executives, customers, and other stakeholders. It is very important for her to learn to master her speaking and conversation skills, so she hired a speech coach who made her aware of her own *umms*, *buts*, *becauses*, and *ands*. Chris says, "I had no idea how often I was doing this. Once someone called it out and I heard myself, I realized that this was not the way I wanted to sound to others." Chris addressed this issue by beginning to play back her voicemails before sending them. Chris says, "When I heard how many *ands*, *buts*, and *umms* I used, or, *you knows*, I became aware of a pattern of speech that I had probably been carrying for years." She says she would rerecord those messages five or six times until her voice was confident and her messages were concise. "This technique has helped me become aware of my speech patterns and to be much more effective in my communications."

Guideline 8: Speak Up! Believe You Deserve to Be Heard

Consider this situation: A critical customer issue has surfaced and you have been called into an emergency meeting to address it. As soon as everyone is seated in the conference room, a colleague jumps right in with her solution to the problem. Others are quick to support it but you're skeptical—maybe you doubt that it's the right fit for your client or perhaps it somehow conflicts with your values. But the momentum of the meeting makes you feel like it would be somehow inappropriate to speak up as the naysayer. Later, when your concerns start to pan out, you call a trusted colleague and confess that you wish you had said something in that meeting and don't know why you didn't.

Or consider this one: In team meetings, you often have ideas or thoughts about a certain project that you're sure would add value to the discussion at hand. You wait for your boss to turn and ask for your input, but he doesn't, and you wind up leaving the meeting frustrated that you didn't get to participate. Worse, later on you realize that your boss or colleagues have made all sorts of assumptions about what your opinions or interests are regarding that particular project. And, they are not accurate.

Clearly you are *a mouse who needs to learn to roar a little*!

These two examples illustrate what happens when fear stops us from speaking up when we really do have something to say. Sometimes it's rooted in a desire to avoid conflict or hurting someone's feelings. Or it can be about risk aversion—the need to avoid being wrong, criticized, or rejected. But silence isn't the safe zone many people think it is. Keeping quiet at the wrong time can make a person seem weak or insecure. Difficult as it may be, at the end of the day, people respect those who speak up to voice their views or concerns.

Speaking up can be especially hard for women because so often as girls we're taught to value being liked, not to garner respect. As adults, we don't want to rock the boat so we defer. Or we speak up near the end of the conversation when the best opportunity to have an impact has passed. Men, on the other hand, have been socialized to be competitive and assertive. In meetings they jump in with their ideas, sometimes just to demonstrate their knowledge to the group.

As I've discussed, being a good listener is critical to communicating effectively. However, perpetual silence doesn't make you seem patient and sage so much as ineffectual and inscrutable. You don't want others to assume they know your point of view so you need to speak up enough to make your intentions, interests, and perspectives known.

Gerri Elliott, a vice president at Microsoft, says, "I will always be the one to bring up the elephant in the room." She points out that people who are ultimately heard are sometimes the ones who raise the topics that no one wants to talk about, but that need to be on the table. "Asserting yourself is harder in certain cultures. And no matter who you are, someone can question your idea," she says. "But it is all about what you know and how you say it."

Women have great ideas and can think through them well. The challenge for us is not being afraid to say them. Learning to assert yourself when it isn't your natural inclination can seem about as easy as learning to not be scared of heights when you are. But everyone can learn to be assertive in certain situations, even if it isn't something that comes naturally to them.

Another barrier for women is that we sometimes spend so much time crafting our message and thinking through the best way and time to talk about it that by the time we are ready and feel comfortable to speak, people have moved on. Or, as many women explain, by the time they are really ready to speak, they are in the car driving home! For many of us, it gets down to the fear that what we say won't be right or it may offend someone. I coach women to speak up in a conversation by using the "throw your hat in the ring" principle. It's all about getting started—getting your voice out there. So, when you have something important to say but you are holding back, try starting out by saying, "I have an idea," or "I would like to make a point," or "I have a question." This is the first step for getting people to pay attention to you and it gets your voice out there. It just takes practice, so try *throwing your hat in the ring* at the next meeting you attend. Know that once you throw your hat in the ring, you will not remain silent. I promise that you will say something, and most likely, it will be brilliant! Just try it!

Following are some key guidelines for speaking up:

1. Act confident, even if you don't feel confident. Believe that you have something to say and focus on the important point of your message.
2. Be current. Have good, relevant information at your fingertips to back up your points or inform the discussion.
3. Be open to constructive criticism. Speaking up is not just about making your point. You need to be receptive and responsive to questions, critical analysis, and commentary on what you're saying and resist feeling defensive or defeated.
4. Balance emotion and logic. Read the emotional dynamics of the conversation and calibrate your message appropriately. Logic does not play well when people have strong emotion-laden opinions or biases.
5. Time your contribution. Follow the dynamics and context of the meeting or conversation before you speak up. Timing and patience have a lot to do with making sure you are heard.

Guideline 9: Decide if You Want to Be Direct and Forthright or Indirect and Subtle

The decision to be forthright or subtle depends on whom you are speaking with and what you want to achieve. Too much of one style and your listeners can feel as though they were hit by a bulldozer; too much of the other and they're not sure at all what you were trying to tell them. Finding the right balance can be difficult, especially if one or the other approach comes more naturally for you.

If you are exceedingly subtle and discreet all the time, and just feel it's too aggressive or pushy to ever be direct, it can limit your ability to demonstrate your leadership by making things happen or by making your wants, needs, or opinions clear. On the other hand, if you are always entirely blunt, you can come across as insensitive or boorish or you can discourage people from engaging you in dialogue—also not a good way to show that you're leadership material.

Anne Altman, managing director, U.S. Federal, IBM Corporation, has often seen managers end meetings without giving their teams clear directives out of a need to be polite. "We fall short in not being more direct or straightforward," she says. For example, a manager might ask, *would you consider doing this?* Whereas, if they know it's what they want, it's okay to be polite but clearer: *I recommend the following and I need your help in getting it done.*

It's possible to be nice without being unnecessarily deferential. Anne observes, "We sometimes use self-deprecating or disempowering disclaimers before we speak. This approach weakens our credibility." If you have a habit of suppressing what you really want to say or you find it hard to step up and provide direction in meetings for the sake of not ruffling feathers, you have a good chance of losing your authority and credibility. It is important to know how to be both forthright and subtle, and to know which one is warranted by the dynamics of a situation. Following are some helpful tips on being both direct and subtle.

Being Direct

1. Avoid "I think." Instead, state your opinion in simple, active sentences, and follow it up with your rationale.
2. Own your message. Once you express a need or an opinion, let it stand. Don't add on a buffer like, "I suppose," or "What do you think?"
3. Avoid turning statements into questions. It makes you sound tentative and makes the listener more likely to doubt you.

Being Subtle

There may be times when you need to draw out the perspective of others, explore possibilities, or ensure that other people feel ownership of some process. All of these are reasons to be more subtle and collaborative. Here are some examples of questions that get your point across clearly but softly.

1. It doesn't seem like we are getting very far in this meeting. What do you say we table this conversation until next week?
2. I'm concerned this contract does not have enough detail. What do the rest of you think?
3. If you were to do this project over again, how would you approach it differently?

Direct Does Not Mean Blunt

A word of caution: While being direct is good in the right instances, some people can unknowingly go overboard. Being overly direct puts others in a defensive mode or they simply will not respond to you for fear of your reply. The result is that you may seem unap-proachable.

I recently had lunch with a woman who was in a tough situation. She was the only woman executive in her organization and felt that to be heard she needed to learn to be very direct. She worked with admirals, engineering types, and other men whose style was more bottom line and get to the point. So she felt, to be heard, she also needed to adapt to that style. But she was noticing that with this new, bolder style, she wasn't fitting in. It turned out that people did-n't know how to respond to her, so they didn't. As we explored her patterns, she realized that she was creating what seemed like a stand-off between her and the men in conversations, and she decided that she might have much better luck by backing off a little. She actually found that, to her amazement, she really didn't need to be strident to make her point or to avoid appearing meek or not confident. She was okay as long as she was direct and not blunt.

To determine whether you are over-directive, be open to how others react or respond to you. You may have something very impor-tant to say, but people may be tuning you out, may react defensively, or may not be sure how to respond to you—so they don't.

Here are some examples which illustrate being blunt versus being direct:

Blunt: These times don't work for me.

Direct: I have a packed day. We need to look at next week.

Blunt: This report was totally off track.

Direct: I had a different expectation of what this report was going to be, so we need to talk.

Guideline 10: Be a Good Facilitator

Albert Einstein is credited with saying, "We can't solve problems by using the same kind of thinking we used when we created them." The best companies today appreciate this idea more than ever and understand that diverse backgrounds and points of view are most likely to generate new thinking. Therefore, one of the most valuable things you can do as a leader is to facilitate communication between the many different people on your team and across your company.

Being able to embrace and connect the multitude of different dots is something that women tend to do well. Male thinking typically is methodical and linear and goes sequentially from one possibility to another. In contrast, women tend toward more integrated thinking—they can hold seemingly different ideas in their heads simultaneously and draw a correlation between them, and they can go back and forth between ideas more easily. You can see how valuable the latter skill would be in a diverse workplace where a meeting can generate all kinds of ideas and the team needs a leader who can coalesce them.

Learning to Connect the Ideas

At IBM, Anne Altman has made a conscious effort to be good at "connecting the ideas." Anne explains, "In our meetings, nobody speaks twice until everyone has spoken. This way we hear all voices, and it balances the extroverts and the introverts." She says that getting all views, including opposing ones, onto the table allows the group to mold them into a collective solution that's usually richer than any one idea would have been on its own. "My view is that meetings are not just to share information, but to see and learn from others," she says.

Anne concedes that keeping a handle on this type of meeting isn't always easy. People can have competing views and occasionally she has to contend with someone who wants to be heard for the sake of it. And the extroverts can still make it hard for others to speak. This is where her facilitation skills come in handy. She explains, "This is when I become a good active listener." To some extent she'll let go and allow others get things out in the open. After the conversation has naturally wound itself down, she'll step up and summarize what she's heard, coalescing all the perspectives, ideas, and concerns. And she'll recommend some kind of action that builds on several of those points. Anne says that this technique lets the others know that she has listened to them, but it keeps the meeting from turning into an exercise in idea-generating for the sake of it that doesn't lead to a conclusion or action.

So being a good communicator can mean being a good facilitator. When something goes wrong, be curious. Connect the diversity of ideas and perspectives into a greater and more innovative solution. Look at ways to draw out those who need and should be heard. See the following sidebar for several tips for when a situation calls for you to be a facilitator.

Tips for Being a Facilitator

1. Use questions to steer parties toward an outcome.
2. Propose ideas by using pros and cons.
3. Point out common patterns among the comments of various parties.
4. Hold off making assumptions until you fully understand where others are coming from.
5. Incorporate views, ideas, and information from several people in your final summation or action plan.

I've covered a lot of important ideas here about communication and using good communication skills to demonstrate your individuality and leadership. No matter how confident or competent we are, being a good communicator gives us a leg up for successfully dealing with the variety of challenges and situations encountered every day. Know that great leadership starts with the power of connection with others. We are naturally great collaborators and connectors. So capitalize on this strength. Be strategic—there is no one way to communicate. Be open and demonstrate the full spectrum of skills, styles, and techniques that will allow you to achieve the result or outcome you are looking for.

You have a voice that needs to be heard. If not, we all miss out.

Chapter 9

Asking for What You Want

Today's Businesses Operate in a World of Collaboration and Negotiation

Today, we live in a world that requires much more collaboration and engagement among peers, bosses, and other key relationships. The world of work is built on partnerships, alliances, and associates. We spend day after day trying to create the best alignment and agreement with the people we work with. In fact, organizations actively recruit good negotiators who know how to ask for what they need to get their job done. This one particular quality, by itself, conveys a sense of confidence and credibility that positively differentiates us from others who don't stand up and ask for what they need.

Gary Budzinski, vice president of Hewlett Packard, said, "Everything you do is somewhat negotiated." "But to do that," Gary said, "you need to communicate your expectations, gain agreement with others and then do what you agreed on. You need to move beyond the *yes sir* or *yes ma'am* and instead, look at *asking for what you want* as an opportunity to create better alignment on an issue." Gary also shared that people appreciate others who take the initiative to do this.

To Gary's point, in today's work environment, women have a strategic advantage when asking for what they want. They are often better able to read and connect with people, which is an essential skill in successful negotiations. "Women need to learn and accept how much influence they really have in the business environment. This is a leverage point for women and an advantage if they use it appropriately."

So Why Is Asking for What We Want So Hard for Us?

It is amazing, yet true, that we still ask for permission to negotiate or ask for what we want! In many cases, what holds us back from not getting what we want is simply not asking for it. This can end up substantially impacting our career potential right down to our financial well-being. Tory Johnson, CEO of Women for Hire, said, "Men are four times more likely to negotiate an offer than women—that leaves $500,000 on the table over the course of a woman's career." Wow, if we only knew how much we were leaving behind, we might think twice about asking.

Pink Magazine found that nearly half of the 2,400 women surveyed had not asked for a raise, additional benefits, or a promotion in the past 12 months. The study also indicated that those who didn't ask missed out, because 72 percent of those who did ask got it! Another interesting statistic indicates that in some cases, others are expecting us to ask and are surprised when we don't. Imagine that! The Society for Human Resources indicated in a recent study that 80 percent of human resource professionals surveyed said that they expect counteroffers from employees when agreeing on salaries. So, if you are considering a new job or feel that you are under compensated, don't rule out the fact that your organization or your boss is willing and able to make that salary adjustment.

So, why is asking for what we want so hard for many of us to do? And, I mean asking for *any* of it—a raise, a promotion, time off, more visibility, additional resources, or something we really feel as though we deserve. I often get asked by women, "Why aren't we at the level of equity that we deserve to be?" Or I will hear, "There's something still wrong with the system" or "we are not seen as valuable as men." Well, in some cases, there is still inequity for women. One example is the continued pay gap, which still indicates that women earn only 80 percent of what their male colleagues do in a similar job. That is an issue that still needs to be addressed. However, I encourage you to look within yourself to see what you are doing that might be holding you back from getting what you want, need, and deserve.

In many ways, we are born to be great negotiators despite some of these statistics showing that we don't negotiate for ourselves. Some of our natural characteristics and traits can actually lead to being a good negotiator because we are good collaborators and tend to keep our egos out of the negotiating process. We are also known for going to bat and asking for more money, promotions, and recognition for other people who we care about. But, rarely do we do that for ourselves.

When I talk with women's groups and at conferences, I find it stunning that we still minimize our accomplishments, and think we still need to ask for permission to ask for what we want. One key reason is that we find it hard to promote ourselves or give ourselves permission to ask for what we really desire. I emphasize with women that it is important to recognize what we are good at and that we deserve something that is important and fair for ourselves. "We are in a place now in the business community where we don't need to be trailblazers." Tory Johnson reemphasized that notion by saying, "The opportunities are here and we are expected to ask for what we deserve."

Christina Hanger, COO of Worksoft, said, "Sometimes we think that everyone should read our minds—that they should just know what we want." But Christina said she started early on in her career thinking that it was okay to ask for what she wanted. What helped her to realize this was when she started to observe that others had gotten opportunities and she asked them how they did it. And they said, "I asked for it." Or, she learned that those getting the choice assignments and opportunities would let someone know they were interested in a certain role or responsibility and in many cases, in a month or so, something similar to their request came up and the organization reached out and offered it to them. Christina added that sometimes we make it more difficult or stressful than it has to be when deliberating over whether we should ask for that raise, bonus, or some other opportunity. Christina said, "For example, there was a time when I knew I was underpaid in my current role, but I didn't want to change companies." She went on to explain that learning about opportunities at other companies made her realize she was underpaid compared to her peers and the marketplace. Rather than wait or assume that her boss would make the adjustment for her, she took the initiative and scheduled some time with her right away. She made her aware of the inequity—simple and to the point. "I didn't ask for anything, just explained the situation. And a few weeks later, I heard from my boss that I was getting an increase in salary. In a few months, at annual bonus time, I received the largest bonus I had at that point in my career." It is important to learn that, like Christina, showing up with a sense of confidence, self-respect, being astute, and letting people know what you know is sometimes all that's needed to get what you deserve. Christina said, "I used to worry about asking for something—now I realize that was my issue and that nothing is lost by asking for what you want. Either you get better results as a result of asking or you don't, which is a valuable form of feedback."

You Don't Get What You Don't Ask For

Lota Zoth, former CFO of MedImmune, said, "I remember the first time in my career when I went out on a limb to ask for something— it was a promotion and I really didn't think I was entitled to it. Since

I was both fearful and uncomfortable in asking, I took time to listen and receive support from several of my colleagues in terms of how to actually ask for the job. Then I took a deep breath and asked. To my surprise, I ended up being offered the position that I had not expected! During my conversation regarding the job offer, I asked for a signing bonus—and yes, I got that too! This was a turning moment for me," Lota said. "I learned that you *don't get what you don't ask for*. Now, if I don't get the title I want, I ask for it. If I don't have the compensation I want, I ask for it. If I don't have the span of control I think I should have, I ask for it."

Lota shared with me that girls often learn early on not to feel entitled to what they want, rather they are socialized to be grateful for what they have. How many times do you hear women say, I am so honored to have this role, so grateful to work for this company? While there is nothing wrong with expressing your appreciation for something, it can work to your disadvantage. Lota said that in the early days of her career, she was grateful for simply getting a paycheck. Women, by our very nature, take things to heart. Later, she began to understand that there are times when you actually have to consciously balance your core value or belief system of being grateful for what you have with boldly taking steps to ask for what you really need or deserve.

Lota said, "It is so important for all of us to become comfortable with asking for what we want because it's no longer like asking for a piece of candy when we were little. The stakes are bigger and have a far greater impact on our self-confidence, financial well-being, quality of life, credibility, and respect we earn from others."

What Gets in the Way of Our Asking for What We Want?

Through discussions in our SHAMBAUGH WILL program and my numerous interactions with both male and female leaders, I have found that this particular area is more difficult for women than it is for men. And, it seems that much of what holds us back starts with our own assumption, our particular internal voice, and our own sense of self-worth. Here are some thoughts, common to many women, that hold us back:

- **Too risky:** Sometimes we are fearful of what support or advice we may receive. For example, say you are looking for a promotion and decide to seek advice as well as support from your mentor. And, in the process, you get a recommendation to explore a job you are not interested in—you really don't want that job but your mentor insists it's perfect for you. What do you do? Risk losing your mentor? Go for it and hope you don't get it?

- **Don't want to be asking for personal favors:** Have you noticed that it is easier to ask for support or help for your team than it is for yourself? We tend to avoid asking for something we need because it may be perceived as asking for special treatment or brown-nosing—being the teacher's pet. It may seem like we are asking for special favors and we certainly don't want to be seen as using that relationship for our personal gain.

- **Overly grateful:** We are so grateful for what we have that we don't want to seem disingenuous or as though we don't appreciate what we have been given.

- **Fear of rejection:** We fear the "no" response and can take it too personally. We think that we will lose something in the relationship if we ask and are turned down.

- **Making assumptions:** We assume our boss thinks that Joe is better than we are, or that this is all they will pay for this job, or that the company won't provide extra time off because "it's not the way they operate around here." We don't test our assumptions and they stop us dead in our tracks.

- **People know what I want**: We think that people know the quality of our work, what we need, and how hard we work. Therefore, they will take care of us.

What seems to get in our way can be addressed if we take time to test our assumptions. In many cases, we learn that we have more control and influence than we thought we did.

What If You Ask and They Say No?

One of the reasons we hold back from asking for what we want is the fear of someone saying no. When coaching women to ask for something, I encourage them to be ready for the possibility of someone saying no. It can be hard to separate the personal from the business side, which can lead us to feeling devalued or even rejected. Rarely is that the case. Know that it is okay to disagree and see things differently and that saying no does not mean that it will always be no. Part of asking for something and getting it is based on timing, other priorities, or how we ask. Sometimes it is simply a matter of the *person you are asking is having a bad day.*

Gary Budzinski, vice president of Hewlett Packard, said that his strategy for getting what he asks for is: *Go to bat three times for what you want.* If he asks the organization for something and they say no, Gary said that's okay. He tries a second time if this is the battle he wants to fight. The organization may still say no. But even after that, he will rethink his strategy and go back again. Why? "It is amazing what a new day or a different time can lend itself to," Gary said. "In some cases, when they say *no* the first and even the second time, it doesn't really mean *no.* It may mean that I didn't present the right data or it wasn't the right time to be asking." So try his three strikes rule. Go back and ask with a different approach or provide different information. Reapproach by saying, "Maybe I did not communicate my request clearly to you," or "I would like to revisit this," or "I have some new information. Would you allow me to explore this with you one more time?"

You can easily determine what you want, but other people don't know it unless you inform them and ask for it. Gary said asking for help is a sign of strength. Some of the best leaders are the ones who are not afraid of asking for what they want. They may not get it the first time, but eventually they will.

It Doesn't Have to Be All or Nothing

I was speaking at a conference in New York recently and a woman executive reached out to me and said she was seriously considering leaving the organization that she had been with for 10 years. She was very close to entering the executive suite as a senior partner. But, she had three children and felt that she needed extra time off from work to deal with the many demands of her family. In particular, she was feeling guilty that she had not been there enough for her children. And, she felt she could not be a good parent based on the demands and constraints of her job. So, she shared with me that she was planning on resigning that month. I then asked the question, "Did you ever consider asking for some time off—maybe even going part-time for a year or so?" She replied that her organization did not allow time off for childcare or part-time sabbaticals at her level. She implied that the organization she worked for is all about getting results. While she made that assumption, I sensed her tremendous frustration and internal conflict based on all the time and energy she had given to her firm and now having to potentially walk away from it. But, I could see that deep down she knew her family was most important. I empathized and respected her value system regarding her family and wanting to be there for them, but said, "It is okay for your career to slow down for a while based on your personal and family needs. But, that does not mean you have to give up your aspirations of being partner in your organization—something you have worked so hard to achieve. Five years from now, you might be in a very different place, with more flexibility in your life, and then you can pick up on your career again. So, it doesn't have to be all or nothing." I suggested that she go to her boss and propose an interim role as a part-time employee and let him know that she would be the best part-time employee they could ever have. I said there was a good chance her boss would appreciate this proposal, as it would be a regrettable loss if the company would lose her 10-plus years of institutional knowledge and expertise, now and in the future. We tend to be so pragmatic sometimes about what exists right now and not see the possibility of the future, particularly when it comes down to what we really want—our hopes and dreams.

What Can You Do Tomorrow?

Remember, people have more respect and will take you more seriously if you define what it is you want and then ask for it. Don't wait for others to determine what is best for you. It is incumbent upon us to be in control of our own destiny!

Following are some steps you can take to help you to start asking for what you want.

1. **Know you are worth it—take stock in you:** Take time to realize how valuable you are and that you bring a lot to the table. Maintain your credibility, be honest with yourself and others, and demonstrate personal integrity by asking for what you deserve.

2. **Research your request or worth:** Don't just assume you are worth it or that someone will take you seriously. Consider multiple sources—industry standards/trends, internal and external market salaries, and other best practices. You also need to consider the other parties' interests, as well as their hot buttons, goals, and assumptions, when asking for what you want. It can be a two-way street.

3. **Be curious—don't jump to assumptions:** Take a collaborative approach. When asking for what you want, avoid being one-dimensional—build a bridge between their concerns and interests and your request. Be curious about their view of the world and how your request can be a win–win solution. Ask open questions to explore their view and use phrases that imply a joint success, such as: How do we both do well? How would you define success? or How can this turn into a win for you? Be careful not to over-question or listen passively for too long. Find the right balance between listening, asking questions, and then getting to the answer. Otherwise, the other person may feel that you implicitly agree with them or that you are more interested in their idea than you are in having them respond to your request.

4. **Figure out what you don't know** and then *build your strategy:* Get the lay of the land to get some context. Avoid going in and just asking first—it's better to engage in an open dialogue to explore the best approach in terms of getting what you want. For example, if you are going in for a promotion say, "I have been in this role for three years. What do you think it would take for me to get the next promotion?" Your boss may say there is a freeze on promotions so "not now" but in six months we can come up with a plan. By using open-ended questions, you can get better information to help you decide what your strategy should be. If you learn that there is a freeze on promotions, then shift your request to something else. Ask for something other than the promotion, or propose the question, "Suppose six months from now things are different, what are my chances?" and "What do I need to do to achieve this goal?" Then, commit to come back in six months and reevaluate.

5. **Have a backup plan**: No matter how good you are about asking for what you want, there may be circumstances that cause people to say *no*. So have a backup plan. Maybe your request is for more money but the answer is . . . there is no money. So, have another alternative. Consider asking for an extra week of vacation, continuing education, a benefit option, or flexibility in your job. That way you won't walk away from the conversation empty handed. *Never put yourself in a position where the response is a final no.*

6. **Use "What if"**: If your boss says you need more visibility in order to advance, then you can say, what if I take on the United Way fund-raising campaign for the company or what if I take a lead role on the transition team for the new company integration? Involve your boss with the "what if" and he or she will gain commitment to your request.

7. **Be patient and flexible**: If you don't get a positive reply or "yes" to your request the first time, don't take it as a *no* or *not interested* from the other person. Exercise patience and give people the opportunity to think about your request. They may need time to run it past someone else or they just may be busy and need time to think about it.

8. **Find your comfort zone**: You may feel comfortable taking the direct approach when asking for what you want and just naturally make your request. That might be your style. However, if you are not as confident in being direct, get someone on your side before you do it. Ask them how they would approach it or identify someone from the outside who will support what you want.

9. **Don't expect others to know what you want**: People can't always read our minds or see all the good work we do.

Sometimes we operate on the notion that if we do a good job, others will notice and take care of or reward us. That's not always the case. Take time to update your boss or your organization on your accomplishments, on the progress you have made toward your development, and on the value you are bringing to them and the organization. Let them know your career desires and goals—don't just assume that they are not interested, don't have time to listen, or won't support you. And, if you ask your boss for a promotion or raise and you get turned down, congratulate yourself on the fact that you actually let your boss know what you want because there is an implied understanding that he or she should consider your request again down the road!

10. **Just do it!** If you have not asked for what you really want recently, just go and do it! By asking, you will start to build your skill and confidence. If you hold off, it only leads to feeling disempowered, de-energized, or frustrated with yourself and others. Know it might be uncomfortable the first time, but consider this similar to when you started going to the gym. You knew you needed to do it and you may not have enjoyed it the first time, but when you went the next time and the next time, it got easier, and then it actually began to feel pretty natural. It's the same for asking for what you want.

Don't assume that you know the answer, or worse yet, the answer is no. Know that people appreciate those who stand up and let them know what they need and want.

The old saying goes, "What's the worst thing that can happen?" So go for it. If we don't ask for what we want, we will never know what we can really have! Good things rarely show up at our front door. Don't hesitate; take time to know why, who, and how to ask.

Chapter 10

Now Is the Time!

WHATEVER YOUR GOALS, whatever your dreams, now is the time to reach for them. Women are poised to take on new roles like never before. Major changes and shifts in the business world and, indeed, society as a whole, are requiring a new balance of knowledge, leadership, and perspective. These changes, combined with the ongoing void of leadership talent, mean companies can no longer ignore 50 percent of the available labor pool who happen to be women. In fact, today many companies have human resource policies and practices that recognize the importance of women in the talent pipeline. These initiatives accommodate the need for better work-life blending (which benefit both men and women). Industry leaders are now looking at the concept of "on and off ramps" to retain female talent in the child-bearing years. Our workplaces need and want the female perspective.

There is no question in my mind that this is the time to find a new and synergistic balance of leadership—integrating and balancing the greatest potential of women and men for catalyzing the right change and to achieve and sustain an economic and social well-being on a global basis. These unique confluences of events—changing policies and a need for different types of leaders—present timely and exciting opportunities for women as we are an important force for that shift and for social change. We naturally possess a great deal of personal knowledge, attributes, and natural characteristics that will be more important in the workplace as time goes on. So, exploit that! This is an opportunity for you to rise to this important time and need.

You Have the Choice...

The world is ready, and we are poised to take on more of a leadership role within our organizations, communities, and the world. What is wonderful is that you have a choice . . . and how empowering that is. There is some degree of reflection that causes me to believe that we always did have the choice, but we just needed to acknowledge it. *Now* we do and we know it! The choices we make will allow us to live our lives on purpose—our purpose, no one else's. Our job is to know what we want and take accountability for getting it.

Helen Thomas, my very dear friend, former White House correspondent, and bestselling author, told me recently, "Today, women journalists enjoy a much higher profile in television and in every newsroom across the country than they ever have had in our history. However, there is still apparent discrimination in the salaries of men and women. But, I think there is hope! Women just need to be more aggressive, more determined, and more courageous in stepping up to the plate and asking for what they deserve."

The value of this book is not as much how to do it, although we talk about tools and techniques. Rather, it is knowing what you want and believing that getting what you want starts with you. Once you believe that you set the foundation to ask and negotiate for what you want, to make your words count, to build and capitalize on your relationships, to move beyond your fears and take the right risks, and to show up as that inspirational and powerful leader who brings her own presence and power to any conversation or situation. You can do it!

Where to Go from Here

After reading this book, I hope you are more aware of your hidden strengths that are ready to be tapped, or limiting behaviors or assumptions that have you caught on a sticky floor. Or perhaps you are better equipped to see and know how to avoid a sticky floor that will limit your potential. I am not asking you to conquer all of the sticky floors. There may be only one that is important to you, your biggest priority, which is worth addressing and working on.

As soon as you do that, you will open yourself up to possibilities. And possibilities are what we are talking about in this book—the possibility of determining what you want, what you want to achieve, what is stopping you, and ways to get unstuck. Whatever it is, know it is in your power to have what you want.

So I leave you with the following recommendations.

Have a Plan

A plan gives you focus and accountability. So, make a plan, and then share the plan with others and get their input. Most of all, be willing and open to reaching out to others and asking for help. Build and capitalize on your *own* board of directors.

Don't Let Your Fears Stop You

Everything is possible. You need to believe and want it. It may be a cliché, but the old adage, "The only thing to fear is fear itself" is true. The number one thing that can hold women back is the fear of failure. Thomas Edison tried thousands of times to invent the light bulb before he finally got it right. So when you feel your fear coming on, ask yourself, what's the worst that can happen? Addressing and walking through our fears is not actually failing, rather it is learning and strengthening our own inner confidence that enables us to take those next steps or leaps of faith for achieving our greatest leadership potential.

We Can Do So Much Together, So Little Alone

Whether it is your desire to get to the executive suite, find a better work/life balance or even take an off-ramp, the most important thing we need to do is be supportive of other women—supporting each other in our dreams and goals and knowing that we can do so much more together than alone. My niece, Nicole, recently said to me, "I would like to think that today's women executives and leaders will help to pave the way for my generation. It is important for me to understand what I need to learn based on their experiences and lessons learned." So consider your legacy in terms of how you helped or coached women coming through the ranks in the next generation. While their sticky floors may be different, it will be important that these young women recognize them before they get stuck.

Don't Wait—Do It Now!

When you look back on your career, how are you going to measure your success? Will it be by achievement, job title, family, money, or just enjoyment? Or perhaps it will be based on how fulfilled and happy you felt in your job or what you gave back. What will your legacy be for helping other women—your daughters and nieces?

Think about how it would feel to get to be 65-years-old and look back and wonder "what if?" What if you had asked for the time off with your family? What if you had gone after that promotion? What if you had taken a risk and decided to leave your current job or profession and try something different—something you were terribly passionate about? Don't wake up one day asking "what if." Don't wait for someone else, your boss or organization, to create your life.

You are your own creator. You live what you believe and want. Everything is possible. You need to believe and want it.

The world is opening the door for you to step in and take on important roles, and to bring a new and important balance of leadership and knowledge to the table. Take charge to create and shape what great things you are intended to do.

Whether it is rising to the executive suite, being the best mother you can be, or reaching out and helping others along the way, realize you have the power and own it! If you feel stuck, or see others who are, remember to look within yourself or encourage others to do the same. It is within your power to get off the sticky floors! Be aware of who you are and know that it is within your own power to know and leverage your strengths and overcome what is stopping you. You then can personally take charge of getting yourself off the sticky floor, and remember when you rise off the sticky floor, the sky is the limit.

Have fun with this—enjoy and be the very best you can be. When you do, you will open up a world of wonderful possibilities.

Appendix

Know Yourself and Your Sticky Floors

WE ONCE BELIEVED that what limited us in our careers was the "glass ceiling"—others preventing us from rising to the top. While that might still hold true in some organizations, it's important for each of us to look at what we might be doing—or not doing—that is also holding us back. I call these the "sticky floors." If you are curious to learn where you fall in the spectrum of the sticky floors, here is an exercise that can help you identify the ones that you want to do something about.

Exercise: Assessing Your Sticky Floors

Work/Life Balance

Work-life balance is knowing and being aware of your values; how they play out in your whole life—both personally and professionally; and being aligned with what those most important values are, so you can live your life accordingly. You need to develop both focus and accountability around your values, and establish boundaries for yourself and others around how you balance your life—because at the end of the day, you are in control of what that work-life balance looks like for you. *Are you focusing on the things in your life right now that really matter to you?*

	Yes	No
1. I feel motivated, energized, and creative at work.		
2. I don't have difficulty saying "no" to others.		
3. I feel on top of my work and not overwhelmed.		

Loyalty Factor—Staying in Once Place Too Long

The loyalty factor is that "boss-centric syndrome" where you've been with a boss and you've got a very close relationship with him or her. That boss has been a very strong supporter for you and you've done great things together. You know that if you just continue to do a good job, things will continue to be great for you. One limitation of this is that you only get one perspective on things—that of your boss—and one source of feedback, when it might be helpful for you to get other input as you are trying to increase your skills and broaden your business perspective.

And with the loyalty factor comes the problem of staying in one job or place too long—you limit your opportunity to self-identify and socialize yourself as an individual throughout the organization. You not only can become cobranded with your boss, but you also limit your ability to broaden your breadth and depth of knowledge and credibility outside of your own domain. Although you may be recognized as being a good number two person, you may in fact not even be noticed. To avoid staying in one place too long, you need to be willing to take risks—stepping out of your comfort zone in a variety of work situations and knowing that you may not be successful initially, is all about learning how to bring greater value over time.

	Yes	No
1. I have a career strategy with an action plan and important milestones to get there.		
2. I consider other career options and new roles without a sense of guilt or loyalty to my boss, team, or organization.		
3. I am open to taking on a new assignment or job, even if it is in an area where I am not totally qualified.		

Perfectionism versus Excellence

Perfectionism is getting things right to a standard that is probably higher than necessary. There are some tasks where you need to perform at very high standards and others that are not as important. We need to know what the critical things are to be putting our energy into and where you can say "this is good enough" and move on.

Over perfectionism can also send out the message that you are not confident in yourself and that you are "overtrying" to get it right.

Perfectionism can also lead to micromanaging and can impact how effective you are at delegating. It can make you overly critical of the work that is being given to you—holding others to your perfectionist standards, which might not be the best for that particular piece of work or situation.

You can miss the broader business perspective and be perceived as a great "doer" but not very strategic or executive-like.

	Yes	No
1. I know the standards of work performance based on the expectation of my key stakeholders and I consciously decide whether I will meet or exceed them.		
2. I don't get caught up in the details of things and lose sight of the bigger picture or broader business perspective.		
3. I do not micromanage others' work to ensure it meets very high standards, and I am not overly critical of others who do not meet my high standards of performance.		

Building Strategic Relationships

Building strategic relationships is having a goal that is important to you, and then looking at those individuals who can help you achieve it rather than doing it on your own. It's looking at what you need to learn, who you need to know, who could be an advocate or sponsor for you, figuring how to contact them, and then being able to ask for that help in a way the people know how to respond. It's also leveraging and building broader and deeper relationships across the organization, and looking at networks of relationships as more of a web than your traditional organizational chart.

	Yes	No
1. I have a diverse group of people in my network which includes individuals in my industry as well as inside and outside my company.		

	Yes	No
2. I don't have a problem asking others for help or support.		
3. I look at ways I can be of value to other key stakeholders, regardless of if I need their support or not.		

Political Savvy

Political savvy is socializing your leadership across the organization. It's learning about who needs to know what, and who needs to know you. It's figuring out the best mechanisms for knowing about what's happening in the organization so you can bring value to situations rather than just hoping that information will come to you.

It's also recognizing the informal influence patterns or connections in the organization, knowing who has whose ear, who the key decision makers are in decisions that are important to you, trying to uncover hidden agendas, and trying to see something from another person's perspective.

It's not always about taking people at their word, but rather "reading between the lines" to understand the intention of their words. It's that situational awareness—paying attention carefully to that environment around you—and determining what organizational and cultural aspects are at play. It's having the right intelligence to know how people are going to respond, how decisions are going to be made, and how the information is really going to flow.

	Yes	No
1. I know who in the organization needs to know about me and my work in order for me to advance in my career.		

	Yes	No
2. I know the formal and informal process for how decisions that are important to me will be made.		
3. I can "read between the lines" and get the real intention of the words in what I read or hear.		

Making Your Words Count

Making your words count means coming into the room fully prepared with the message you want to deliver and having that message relevant enough that it resonates with the audience—whether that's an individual or a group, formal or informal setting, etc. It's not filling the room with words, but giving a clear, concise message, and owning that message—staying on it. It's not rambling. It's presenting relevant facts and quantifying statements when that kind of data has greater impact than just making statements. It's showing that you've done your homework.

It's also speaking up. We need to speak up when we have something important to say.

Being able to read the other person or the audience is critical to making your words count because that kind of "intelligence" helps you determine how to adapt or modify your message to achieve your goal.

	Yes	No
1. My messages are clear and concise—I don't ramble on about something to make my point.		

	Yes	No
2. I insert my voice and am heard when I have something to say.		
3. I consider what I want the result to be of my important communications/conversations and frame my message accordingly.		

Asking for What You Want

Knowing and asking for what we want is something we are entitled to and others expect us to do. We sometimes think that others can read our minds and respond to what we want. Or we are sometimes fearful of being turned down or being seen as too pushy and not appreciative of what we have already.

And, we may ask for help, but we ask in a way that people don't know how to respond. We are not thinking through what it is that we want that person to do, so we really need to look at how we are framing the request for help.

It's planning ahead and determining who the right people are to ask for this particular help. Who has the right information or connections or expertise . . . and who can I trust?

It's also following up to let someone know the value of the help they gave you. It's thanking them.

Finally, it's important to recognize that when you do ask people for help, they have the right to say no, so you don't fall into the realm of manipulation.

	Yes	No
1. I begin with the assumption that others will be open and responsive to my requests.		

	Yes	No
2. I think about how I am going to ask for help in terms of exactly what I want from that person.		
3. I feel comfortable asking for what I want versus waiting for someone else to respond to my needs.		

References

Catalyst Consulting Group; Lexington, MA 2006 Perspective—Catalyst Releases 2005 Census of Women Board Directors and Corporate Officers, August 2006

George, Bill and Peer Sims, "Discovering Your Authentic Leadership," *Harvard Business Review,* February 1, 2007, pp. 3–5.

Center for Creative Leadership; Greensboro, NC

Nash, Laura and Howard Stevenson, *Just Enough*, Hoboken, New Jersey: Wiley & Sons, Inc., 2004

Forbes Magazine listed Sharon Allen as one of The 100 Most Powerful Women. August 31, 2006

Law.com's In-House Counsel, Commentary: Relocating—with Eight Kids—for Dream In-House Job, by Wendy Hufford, Corporate Counsel, May 14, 2007

Ibarra, Herminia and Mark Hunter. "How Leaders Create and Use Networks" *Harvard Business Review* , January 1, 2007, p. 2

Fiorina, Carly. *Tough Choices: A Memoir.* New York: Penguin Group, 2006

Goleman, Daniel. *Emotional Intelligence.* New York, Bantam Books, 2006

Thompson, Chic. *What a Great Idea 2.0.* New York, HarperCollins, 2007

Brizendine, M.D., Louann. *The Female Brain.* New York, Broadway, 2006, page 5.

Merrill, Dr. David. *Personal Styles and Effective Performance*, CRC Press, 1999, page 60.

Pink Magazine cited for "Pink Magazine found…" cited on Tory Johnson's Web site www.womenforhire.com

Chapter Reminders— How to Take Action

A previous exercise in this book was intended to help you to identify one or several sticky floors you may want to address. Here is a summary of some key techniques and tools to consider to avoid getting stuck, for getting unstuck, or for coaching others of the sticky floors.

Chapter 1: Know Yourself—Be Yourself

- Know Your Heart
  - Personal beliefs
  - Values
  - Motivators
- Know Your Mind
  - Areas of expertise
  - Knowledge
  - Skills
  - Strengths and weaknesses
- Know Your Dreams
  - Short term and long term goals
  - Hopes and fears
  - Immediate intentions

Chapter 2: Taking Action for Knowing and Being Yourself

- Compare your strengths and weaknesses to those needed in the executive suite and create your own development plan
- Use a 360-degree feedback assessment at work and/or systematically solicit feedback to assess your knowledge, skills, and abilities as perceived by others
  - Identify the behaviors and attributes that matter
  - Determine who can really provide meaningful feedback
  - Solicit feedback in a variety of ways
  - Develop an action plan and review it with mentors

- Update Your Belief Systems
  - Reassess what is right/wrong, good/bad, not working for you at this point in your life
  - Determine how your beliefs are impacting your self-image
  - Reframe your beliefs

- Assess Your True Values
  - Decide what success looks like to you personally and professionally
  - Identify the core values that mean the most to you
  - Set priorities
  - Live your values consistently in your "whole" life

- Create Your Personal Vision
  - Determine what you truly want—now and in the future
  - Ask for what you want and need!
  - Stretch your thinking from short term to long term

- ***Tools: Create Your Lifeline, Update Your Belief System, Assess Your Values, Create Your Personal Vision***

Chapter 3: Balancing Your Work and Life

- Recognize Work/Life Balance as Your Sticky Floor
  - Exhaustion all the time
  - Anger with "short temper"
  - Feelings of "burn out"
  - Lack of creative spark
  - Lack of motivation

- Look for Syndromes
  - Multitasking—Are you trying to do too many things at the same time?
  - Martyr—Are you feeling guilty that you're letting others down?
  - Self-critical—Are you feeling that nothing is ever good enough?
  - Perfectionist—Are you trying to be the best at everything?

- Determine *Your* Elements of Success in Life
  - Happiness—having feelings of pleasure and contentment
  - Achievement—having accomplishments you are proud of
  - Significance—having a positive impact on people that matter to you
  - Legacy—passing along your values or way of doing things in ways that help others find future success

- Check Your Personal Keys to Success
  - Self-awareness
  - Humility
  - Realistic expectations
  - Diverse interests
  - Leadership

- Write Your Action Plan
  - Get focused
  - Establish and communicate your boundaries
  - Build and use your support network
  - Start now!

- *Tools: Wheel of Life, 5 Keys to Work/Life Balance*

Chapter 4: Embracing Good Enough

- Recognize Perfectionism as Your Sticky Floor
  - In your own work habits
  - In your management of others (micromanaging)
  - In your responsiveness to others in the organization
  - In the perceptions your are creating about your potential

- Determine Where Your Need Comes From
  - Your nature
  - Your family and life experiences
  - Your socialization as a woman

- Look for the Signs
  - Second guessing yourself
  - Always needing more input to be certain
  - Being perpetually dissatisfied with the work others do
  - Assuming no one can do it as well as you
  - Being adverse to taking on new things that are out of your comfort zone
  - Having a low tolerance for mistakes of any kind
  - Being stopped by the fear of failure
  - Having a strong need to please others

- Assuming everyone has the same high standards as you
- Micromanaging the work of others

- Measure the Negative Impact
  - Appear too mired in details
  - Seen as more of a doer than a leader
  - Seem overworked and in "frantic activity"
  - Appear less confident in yourself and your team
  - Seem overly critical, defensive, risk adverse
  - Appear unresponsive to sense of urgency
  - Appear to be less effective developing and empowering others

- *Tool: Eight Steps to "Good Enough"*

Chapter 5: Making the Break

- Recognize Making the Break as Your Sticky Floor
  - Staying in one job too long
  - Not wanting to leave your team
  - Being irreplaceable to your boss with little other exposure or recognition throughout the organization
  - Fearing to apply for or take a new position
  - Limiting your career options

- Realize the Truths versus Myths about Unconditional Loyalty
  - Most people *don't* follow traditional career paths anymore
  - Hard work and good performance *are not* the only criteria for getting to the top
  - Relying on one mentor or sponsor *can* limit your opportunities

- What you are being recognized for today *won't* necessarily get you a promotion
- Years of successful experience in your position *won't* give you a competitive advantage over other candidates vying for the top jobs

- Take Another Look
  - Check your readiness for a job change
  - Lay the groundwork for future moves by networking and making your work/accomplishments, skills, and interests known to others
  - Talk to your boss about your future prospects
  - Begin to groom your successor
  - Continually check your marketability

- Don't Be Afraid to Take the Leap!
  - Get out of your comfort zone
  - Identify your real fears about making a change
  - Figure out what you really want
  - Assess the true risks and rewards
  - Consult with people you respect and trust

- Put Together a Plan
  - Fight the urge to be complacent or to procrastinate and write the plan today!
  - Do your own strategic job analysis—what do you want to do? Next job? Job after that? What do you want to be doing five years from now? 10 years from now?
  - What will it take on your part to get your ideal job?
  - Schedule conversations about your career with others
  - Explore other opportunities to . . . take a leap of faith!

Chapter 6: Forming Your Own Board of Directors

- Consider Three Kinds of Business Relationships
  - *Operational Network*—people who can help you do your job and manage your internal responsibilities
  - *Personal Network*—people who help you learn and develop in your profession beyond your day-to-day work-like professional associations, alumni groups, or personal interest committees
  - *Strategic Network*—people who have a broader business perspective and contacts that can help you better achieve both personal and organizational goals—now and in the future

- Identify Your Own Personal Board of Directors
  - People you respect and trust
  - People who care about you and your success
  - People who have different business/career perspectives
  - People who can be a "connector" for you
  - People who have a greater knowledge of an area than you do
  - People who can influence others on your behalf
  - People both inside and outside your organization

- Actively Build Your Networks
  - Identify people to connect or reconnect with now
  - Identify desired outcomes for each engagement
  - Identify the best way to approach each individual
  - Address any fears that might stop you
  - Consider the Law of Reciprocity—how can you help the other person?
  - Pursue the relationship with integrity, intention, and authenticity

- Remember "Six Degrees of Separation" and ask for referrals
- Seek the kindness of strangers
- Put together a plan for expanding your network
- Start now! Don't wait until you need them
- Follow up after each call or meeting

- *Tools: Sizing Up Your Network, Growing Your Strategic Network*

Chapter 7: Capitalizing on Your Political Savvy

- Recognize Political Savviness as Your Sticky Floor
  - Do people seek you out for information?
  - Do you know how and when most key decisions are made?
  - Are you seldom surprised by events or announcements?
  - Can you "read between the lines" in meetings and conversations?
  - Do you know when to "jump in" and when to "walk away?"
  - Do you have executive presence?
  - Are you viewed as a leader or potential leader?
  - Do people want to spend time with you?

- Develop Your Social Intelligence
  - Learn how to read situations
  - Become fluent in non-verbal cues
  - Tune into your empathy
  - Develop a sense of timing
  - Spend time connecting with people

- Assess and Develop Your Executive Presence
  - Consider your: Candor, Clarity, Openness, Passion, Poise, Self-Confidence, Sincerity, Thoughtfulness, and Warmth
  - Conduct your own personal dress rehearsal before big meetings or events and be sure your team is "on board" with you
  - Observe those that show up with good executive presence

- Market Yourself
  - Share your uniqueness and your accomplishments
  - Speak with an authentic sense of passion and enthusiasm
  - Tell stories about your experiences
  - Develop and practice using your personal "elevator speech"
  - Practice "grateful gratitude" in response to compliments

- *Tools: Assess Your Executive Presence*

Chapter 8: Making Your Words Count

- Recognize Making Your Words Count as Your Sticky Floor
  - Are you clear, concise, and easy to understand?
  - Do you easily adapt your speaking style to the situation and the individual?
  - Do you check yourself on how much or little detail to provide?
  - Do you plan what you are going to say and how you will say it?
  - Do you never hesitate to speak up when you have something of value to say?
  - Do you influence others by what you say, when, and how you say it?

- Follow these guidelines:
  - Capitalize on non-verbal communication (body language) to "hear" both the content and feelings of what is being said and to convey alignment in your own messages
  - Become an active listener to show you are truly trying to understand another person
  - Plan your message by determining the results you want to achieve and the key points you need to make
  - Keep it simple and stay on your message
  - Leverage the use of questions
  - Adapt your style to your audience
  - Pay attention to your speaking habits
  - Speak up! Believe that you deserve to be heard
  - Decide if you want to be direct (forthright) or indirect (subtle)
  - Be a good facilitator

- *Tool: Preference Checklist: Driver, Expressive, Amiable, Analyst*

Chapter 9: Asking for What You Want

- Recognize Asking for What You Want as Your *Sticky Floor*
  - When was the last time you *asked* for a raise or promotion?
  - Do you communicate your expectations to your team members up front?
  - Do you take the initiative to tell others what you want and need—like more visibility, time off, or additional benefits?
  - Do you ask for specific assignments or projects and feel free to say no to others?

- Do you ask for what you want rather than for what you think you can get?

- Consider What Stops You From Asking
  - You feel it's too risky because you don't know what the answer will be
  - You don't want to ask for personal favors
  - You are so grateful for what you have that you don't think you can ask for more
  - You fear rejections—the dreaded "no"
  - You make assumptions that imply you shouldn't ask
  - You think others should know what you want without having to ask for it

- Try This
  - Know you are worth it—take stock in yourself
  - Research your request and determine your value equation
  - Be curious—don't jump to conclusions
  - Build your strategy for asking—most desired outcome, goal, response to anything less than your goal, etc.
  - Have a back-up plan
  - Use the "what if" in response to anything less than your goal
  - Be patient and flexible
  - Find your comfort zone—direct or indirect
  - Don't expect others to know what you want
  - Just do it—ask for what you want!

Chapter 10: Now Is the Time!

- The world is opening the door for you to step in and bring a new balance of leadership to the table

- If you feel stuck, know it is within you to look within yourself—you have the power to get off the sticky floor
- Make a plan that gives you focus and accountability—share that plan with others and get their input
- It starts with you—determine what you want, what you want to achieve, and what is holding you back
- You have a choice—know it is in your power to have what you want

Index

About the Author

Rebecca Shambaugh is the founder, president, and CEO of SHAMBAUGH Leadership, which was recently selected by *Entrepreneur* magazine as one of the top entrepreneurial companies in the Washington, D.C. area. She began her career as a human relations specialist at General Motors and has worked for several major corporations.